PORTRAIT OF THE
ISLE OF WIGHT
RAILWAYS

HANDEL KARDAS

IAN ALLAN
Publishing

First published 1998

ISBN 0 7110 2574 6

Published by Ian Allan Publishing

an imprint of Ian Allan Publishing Ltd, Terminal House, Station Approach, Shepperton, Surrey TW17 8AS. Printed by Ian Allan Printing Ltd at its works at Riverdene, Molesey Road, Hersham, Surrey KT12 4RG.

Code: 9806/B

Front cover:
No W21 *Sandown* heads a Ryde Pier Head-Cowes service between Ryde St Johns and Smallbrook Junction on 21 September 1962. *K. L. Cook/RAS*

Back cover, top:
The 'new' order at Brading on 13 July 1939 as unit No 483001 forms the service from Ryde. *Brian Morrison*

Back cover, bottom:
Restored to SR livery with an original style bunker No 24 *Calbourne* steams past the original station building at Ashey in April 1995. *Stuart Duddy*

Previous page:
Reflections on the wet sand at Ryde on the evening of 19 June 1965, as an 'O2' heads a Cowes-Pier Head train along the pier at low tide. *M. Dunnett*

Below:
'O2' No 26 *Whitwell*, hurrying a train towards Ryde. *Ian Allan Library*

Note on Picture Credits
Where known, the photographer's name is given. In other cases, where pictures have been taken from a picture library or photographic collection, the source is acknowledged. All uncredited pictures are by the author. Abbreviations used in picture credits are:

IAL	*Ian Allan Library*
Bucknall Coll	*The Bucknall Collection*
Madgwick Coll	*The Madgwick Collection*
LGRP	*Locomotive & General Railway Photographs*
LPC	*Locomotive Publishing Co (Including Real Photographs)*

Contents

Bibliography 3

Foreword 5

Introduction 6

1 **Isle of Wight Railway History** 9

2 **Locomotives** 29

3 **Rolling Stock** 55

4 **The Routes** 65

5 **The Electric Era** 99

6 **The Preserved Line** 105

7 *Envoi* 109

Below:
An 'O2' No 31 leaves Ryde St Johns Road
with a southbound train.
Ian Allan Library

Bibliography

A Locomotive History of Railways on the Isle of Wight, D. L. Bradley, Railway Correspondence & Travel Society, 1982

A Pictorial Record of Southern Locomotives, J. H. Russell, Oxford Publishing Co, 1991

Isle of Wight Album, G. M. Kitchenside, Ian Allan, 1967

Isle of Wight Railways (a 'then & now' pictorial survey), Colin A. Pomeroy, Silver Link Publishing, 1991

Isle of Wight Steam Passenger Rolling Stock, R. J. Maycock & M. J. E. Reed, Oakwood, 1997

Once Upon a Line... (four vols), Andrew Britton, Oxford Publishing Co

Rails in the Isle of Wight, P. C. Allen and A. B. MacLeod, David & Charles, 1986

The Island Terriers, M. J. E. Reed, Kingfisher Railway Publications, 1989

Bluebell News, Bluebell Railway Preservation Society — reports in various mid-1960s issues

Railways/Railway World, monthly journal, Ian Allan Publishing — various issues 1950-95

(The above are the main works consulted, all recommended for further reading. Innumerable references to the island's railways can be found in other periodicals and in many books on railway history in general and the Southern system in particular.)

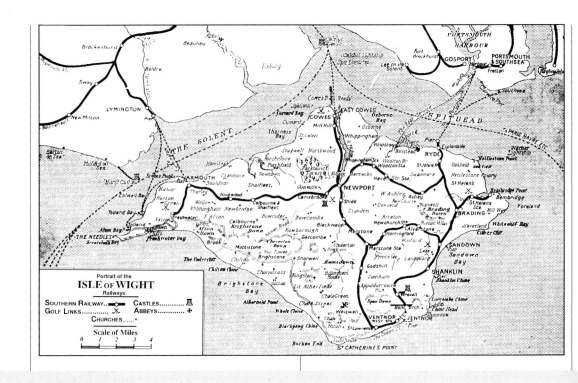

Portrait of the
ISLE OF WIGHT
Railways

SOUTHERN RAILWAY..   CASTLES............. ♜
GOLF LINKS............. ✕   ABBEYS............. ✠
      CHURCHES......+

Scale of Miles
0   1   2   3   4

Foreword

Portrait of the Isle of Wight Railways

A portrait is an image, an impression, of its subject, bearing the artist's interpretation as much as objective reality. So, in creating this *Portrait of the Isle of Wight Railways*, I have not set out to produce a definitive history (that has already been done and to write another would take more patience than I possess) but rather to recapture in words and pictures some of the life and character of this extraordinary little outpost of the British railway system. I have aimed to show something of the uniqueness that made the railway — and makes its surviving sections — so fascinating to so many people.

I have looked at the history of the system, for there is the key to what the visitor was to see; and at its routes and its stock. But not at the people of the line, for that would require a far bigger book to do them justice, justice which has already been done by Andrew Britton in his four-volume *Once Upon a Line*. If, by contrast to that work, I appear to be dismissive of, or unimpressed by the efforts and dedication of the officers and staff of the railways, let me say now that it is not so. Nobody can study the story of the Isle of Wight's 55-mile system without forming the greatest admiration for those who, for 140 years, have done so much to ensure that the island should have a working railway; particularly the engineering staff who, at times when resources were short, support was lacking and morale was suffering, still worked miracles to keep it all running, though their task might be likened to nailing a blancmange to the ceiling!

To many people the Isle of Wight Railways are synonymous with 'O2' tank engines and Southern Region green bogie coaches. But that is to overlook a long history where far more variety could be found. The 18 years of BR steam (and now 30 years of BR electrics) and 25 of the Southern Railway were preceded by 60 years of small and generally impoverished companies struggling valiantly to maintain and improve services. In balancing the content of the book, I have tried to ensure that this early and now largely forgotten era gets the attention it deserves.

In considering the locomotive history, I have used tractive effort as one way of making comparisons between engines. I do not wish to give the impression that I believe that tractive effort is in any way a definitive 'tablet of stone' of a locomotive's power. But treated cautiously, it does at least give a relative figure for the theoretical ability to start a train and get it moving. Treated as an arbitrary calculation that gives some indication of power, it has some value and I suggest that it offers a handy thread to follow through the maze of IoW locomotive development.

No book is one person's unsupported work. I offer grateful thanks first to Peter Waller and Alan Butcher at Ian Allan Publishing; the former first proposed the book and both weighed in with alarmingly large folders of photographs and other material, gleaned from the Ian Allan Library and personal archives. My thanks also to the Isle of Wight Steam Railway for help with material, and especially to the photographers who responded to my appeals for particular subjects, all couched, I fear, in the usual writer's attitude that if I ask for something today it is because I need it yesterday! Thanks also to Dr Fred Youell for his personal memories; I had had these on file for some time and found them at just the right moment while looking for something else — serendipity at full regulator.

Finally, full and grateful acknowledgement to those authors who have been there before, so to speak, and to whose works I have referred in writing this book. They are duly listed in the bibliography.

Above left:
Map of the Isle of Wight railways.

Left:
An Isle of Wight Central Railway train leaves Sandown for Newport, during the 1910s. Beyer Peacock 2-4-0T No 4 heads the train, with the first two coaches being the pair of Lancaster C&W Co bogie vehicles bought in 1889. *LPC*

Introduction

Portrait of the Isle of Wight Railways

What is the appeal of the Isle of Wight Railways? Perhaps it is that for many they are inextricably associated with going on holiday. Getting there in the first place and perhaps exploring the island during one's stay; for a long time, if you went on holiday to the Isle of Wight, as many tens of thousands did every year, you almost inevitably went by train.

For others, particularly railway enthusiasts, there was more. On the one hand there was this smart and smartly-operated little system, moving almost impossible numbers of people between the ferries and the resorts and doing it with considerable panache. On the other hand the whole operation has been, for the whole of this century, not just a dose of nostalgia but verging on an anachronism. It always seems to operate with the equipment of at least a

generation ago. Early in the century its mixed bag of locomotives, all past the first flush of youth and hauling coaches that had vanished elsewhere years before, captivated the youthful P. C. Allen, Hamilton Ellis and their contemporaries. Between the wars it recalled the railways of the late Victorian and Edwardian eras and in the 20 years from the end of World War 2 to the end of steam, it was, for all the modern

Below:
Ryde St Johns Road motive power depot on 15 April 1965, with six 'O2s' standing outside the SR-built running shed. Nos 29 *Alverstone* (left) and 30 *Shorwell* (right) can be identified. *Andrew Muckley*

liveries, quite unmistakably a little pre-Grouping pocket, where small tank engines still hurried around single-line secondary routes with trains of panelled, non-corridor coaches, for all the world as if 40 years of transport history had never happened.

If we are switching alarmingly between past and present tenses, it is of course because not all the Isle of Wight Railways' story is in the past. Just over seven miles of the old system remain as part of the national railway network and carry on this tradition of nostalgia. Only now it is not a long-lost fragment of the steam age that is retained here but a piece of the London Underground. The electrified rump of the system is now on its second generation of second-hand multiple-units bought from London Transport on withdrawal from their original lines. Step onto a train at Ryde Pier Head now and you travel in a 60-year-old tube train originally built to link the City of London with its northern suburbs. Somehow the past and the present are rather hard to untangle when dealing with the Isle of Wight Railways, especially when you remember the successful preservationists at the Isle of Wight Steam Railway. They not only share a station with the electric line, they are also steadily pushing the frontiers of their timescale further and further back from the 1960s, portrayal of which was their original aim. They can convincingly represent the early 1930s now — how much further back will they get?

Independence has always been a feature of the island system. Showing in various ways, it has contributed to the unique and attractive atmosphere. From 1923 to the present day, it has taken the form of more autonomy than you would expect such a small system to have from its big owners. The Island Assistant, in practice a local general manager, was a significant position in the SR hierarchy and established a tradition of semi-freehanded management which has lasted to the present day; on the other hand, the workshops at Ryde (and once Newport too) were expected to maintain and repair their stock to high standards without troubling main works too often. And they did; the achievement of keeping active a fleet of Victorian tank engines and Edwardian coaches to work an intensive service in the 1960s should not be belittled.

Before 1923 the 55 miles of the system were owned and operated by three separate companies (plus the LSWR/LBSCR joint section between Ryde St Johns Road and Pier Head) who, though their survival and improvement was always difficult, sometimes a real struggle, were not prepared to combine into a single concern. Perhaps personalities and local politics were at work but it certainly meant that a unique pocket of railways was maturing on the island, which in 1923 needed prompt and positive action by the Southern to survive. The SR's success in turning round this rather mixed bag of assets was seen in the way the system was able to cope with the increasing demands made on it each summer, regularly being re-equipped and receiving investment, but never actually getting up to date.

The remaining stub of the system continues to play an important part in the island's transport and the preserved section is increasingly good at recapturing the past. Long may they continue in their respective roles, for they are keeping alive a fine tradition of service, always slightly idiosyncratic and definitely something quite unique in British railway history.

Left:
The first locomotives on the island railways were a pair of 2-2-2WTs built for the Cowes & Newport Railway. Near the end of its life, one of the pair (probably No 1 *Pioneer*) brings a Sandown-Newport train into Merstone at about the turn of the century. *IAL/Bucknall Coll*

Centre left:
The C&N, the island's first railway, became part of the Isle of Wight Central in 1889. IWCR No 5, one of the company's Beyer Peacock 2-4-0Ts, stands at Newport station with a typical train of assorted four-wheel coaches. *IAL/Bucknall Coll*

Below:
The Portsmouth-Ryde ferry has long been the most popular route for visitors to the island. In this 1926 view from the pierhead two SR paddle steamers (ex-LBSC/LSWR joint) pass on their trips to (left) and from Portsmouth. *IAL/Madgwick Coll*

Right:
Ventnor, the Isle of Wight Railway's southern terminus, opened in 1866. This Edwardian view shows the station's site, literally quarried out of the chalk downland. One train has just arrived at the island platform; while its passengers cross to the main platform by the 'drawbridge', a second train is leaving for Ryde. The turntable that served as the engine release can just be seen, bottom right. *IAL/Bucknall Coll*

Isle of Wight Railway History

Portrait of the Isle of Wight Railways

Until the middle of the 19th century the Isle of Wight was rather an isolated social backwater of small rural communities. Split from the English mainland in the destructive late phases of the last Ice Age, its importance had since been the strategic one of giving a wide but relatively sheltered sea channel, the Solent, to the South Coast's two great natural harbours, Southampton and Portsmouth.

With, from Tudor times, the Royal Navy steadily giving more importance to its base at Portsmouth, the strategic importance of the island increased, but only as a barrier. Its 150-odd square miles were separated from the mainland by some two to three miles for much of the Solent's length, too far for the Navy to wish to develop it as part of the Portsmouth complex, other than placing a few artillery batteries on it and in Spithead, the channel

lying between Ryde and Portsmouth. Superannuated officers might retire there and it had its share of landed gentry, but otherwise the island progressed slowly, several decades behind the mainland.

Queen Victoria changed all that. She disliked the seaside home she inherited, her uncle George IV's Royal Pavilion in Brighton, where society crowded round as closely as London and the ordinary populace was forever gawping at the windows. With the Prince Consort Albert, she chose to build a new coastal retreat on the Isle of Wight — Osborne House near East Cowes. Its large grounds kept society and the lower classes at bay, even though the island promptly became the smart place to have a country retreat if you could afford it, or to hire a house for the summer if you could not. Holiday weeks for the masses came later.

This sudden uplift in fortunes led to a desire to improve the island's amenities; transport in particular was in desperate need of modernising and in the mid-19th century this could only mean railways. There followed a 40-year period of promotion and construction, modest by national British standards perhaps but quite remarkable for a small island with a sparse population.

The first two lines made the soundest sense in business and transport terms. Railway development began with the Cowes & Newport Railway, enacted in 1859 and opened in 1862. It ran roughly parallel with the River Medina, from the port of Cowes at its mouth, for 4½ miles to Newport at the limit of navigation, the island's administrative centre and the nearest place of any size to its physical centre. Within two years it was followed by the Isle of Wight (Eastern) Railway from Ryde to Shanklin, extended in 1866 to Ventnor. The 'Eastern' part of the title was soon quietly dropped but it defined the geographic location that made the company the most successful of the pre-Grouping railways on the island. Ryde was fast emerging as the main port for passengers to the island, and Sandown and Shanklin, with their fine beaches, were developing as holiday resorts. Ventnor was not far behind, although smaller and more select.

From Brading there was a short branch to Brading Harbour. In 1882 the Brading Harbour Improvement & Railway Co extended this into a fully-fledged branch line serving St Helens docks and Bembridge. The IWR worked the branch from the outset, purchasing it in 1898.

This was one of the IWR's two aberrations. It was never busy and was to be an early loss to the network, but at the time, with St Helens an important goods harbour — most of the island's early locomotives arrived that way — it made sense. It even had a train ferry connection to the LBSCR's Hayling Island branch for a few years in the 1880s but using that route was such a performance compared to the Portsmouth-Ryde ferry that it was doomed to failure.

The other aberration was that the Ryde terminus was at St Johns Road, some three-quarters of a mile from the seafront and Ryde Pier, where the Portsmouth boats docked. As the pier itself was half a mile long (it had to be, to reach water deep enough for the boats at low tide), passengers faced a considerable journey between the pierhead and St Johns Road.

The problem was money, of course. The IWR had limited capital and was not awash with revenue. The cost of building to the esplanade, to

say nothing of extending out to the pierhead, was quite beyond its means; indeed when that link was finally built, it proved to be one of the most expensive parts of the system — and one with high maintenance costs.

This did nothing to comfort the railway's patrons however. Partial relief came in the form of a horse tramway added to the east side of the pier and extended through the streets to St Johns Road, giving a form of rail connection, if not a particularly quick or high-capacity one.

The next line on the scene was the Isle of Wight (Newport Junction) Railway and its early history was an unheeded warning on the risks of railway building on a rural island. It was inspired partly by the belief that a direct link from the Cowes & Newport to the fast-growing east coast resorts would allow Cowes to compete successfully with Ryde as the main port of arrival on the island; a belief which failed to appreciate the power of the vested interests that were promoting the Portsmouth-Ryde route. The nine-mile line was authorised in 1868. The promoters could surely never have dreamed, even in their worst

nightmares, that it would take 11 years to complete.

Running south from Newport to Merstone, the new line then turned eastwards and meandered to Sandown, where the IWR's station became a junction. It was built on the cheap — too much so. Sandown to Horringford was the first section that the IW(NJ)R Co optimistically thought was ready for opening, in 1872. To the directors' horror, Col Yolland of the Railway Inspectorate emphatically disagreed! He turned it down flat, largely on account of the poor quality of the rails. These had been bought secondhand from the LSWR and had already been turned once (ie both sides of the railhead had been used and were worn) and the ends were poor. Other imperfections damned the line in the Colonel's eyes.

His colleague Col Smith was not much better pleased when invited to make a second inspection two years later. The rails had been replaced but the trackbed and rolling stock did not impress him: he too found that the line fell below the minimum standards required for public operation and forbade opening. Col Smith returned the following February, inspecting in addition the Horringford-Shide section, and to the huge relief of the by now frantic company, reported that it was safe to operate and could open.

In August 1875 it was Col Hutchinson's turn, this time to inspect the 1½ miles from Shide to Pan Lane on the outskirts of Newport. Again

		10 50			11 20				11 40		12 20			12 40			13 10	
Ship	Portsmouth Harbour .... d																	
	Clarence Pier .... d				11q00					12q00							12q50	
	Ryde Pier Head .... a	11 15			11 45			12 05			12 45			13 05			13 35	
Ryde Pier Head .... d		11 20	11 35		11 50		12 05		12 20	12 35		12 50	13 05		13 20	13 35		13 50	14 05
Ryde Esplanade ¶ .... d		11 22	11 37		11 52		12 07		12 22	12 37		12 52	13 07		13 22	13 37		13 52	14 07
Ryde St. John's Road .... d		11 26	11 41		11 56		12 11		12 26	12 41		12 56	13 11		13 26	13 41		13 56	14 11
Brading .... d		11 33	11 48		12 03		12 18		12 33	12 48		13 03	13 18		13 33	13 48		14 03	14 18
Sandown .... d		11b40	11b55		12b10		12b25		12b40	12b55		13b10	13b25		13b40	13b55		14b10	14b25
Shanklin .... a		11 44	11 59		12 14		12 29		12 44	12 59		13 14	13 29		13 44	13 59		14 14	14 29
Ventnor Bus Terminal .... a		12 20			12 50				13 16			13 46			14 26	14 26		14 56	14 56

permission was refused and it was not passed until the autumn. There remained just a quarter-mile to bring the line into Newport station but this included the crossing of the Medina Valley, with its curved viaduct linking to the Newport-Ryde line (a later project which had beaten the Newport Junction to completion) and a drawbridge over the river itself. The company's position was now so desperate that it took almost four years for this final link to be opened. Local people might be prepared to make a quarter-mile hike across Newport to change trains but no holidaymaker would and the company's shareholders could only look on wretchedly as the Portsmouth-Ryde crossing and the IWR established themselves as the popular route from the mainland to Sandown and Shanklin. By the time the final link opened in 1879 (yet again after two inspections), the prospect of Cowes-Sandown becoming a major holiday route was doomed. Small wonder that the company failed and went into receivership the following year.

By this time another line was already complete. The Ryde & Newport Railway, authorised in 1872, opened in 1875. It and the Cowes & Newport formed a joint committee to operate their lines and the receiver of the IW(NJ)R handed his impoverished baby into their care. Together they were to amalgamate into the Isle of Wight Central Railway in 1889, the largest of the island's pre-Grouping companies but not the most prosperous. The burgeoning holiday traffic kept that trophy firmly with the IWR.

The Ryde & Newport met, but did not join, the IWR line at Smallbrook, from where the two single lines ran parallel on a shared formation to the St Johns Road terminus. But the solution to the gap between there and the pier was by now being provided, by the two mainland companies who had most to gain from increased holiday and other traffic to the island — the LSWR and the LBSCR.

These two companies had fought bitterly over the Portsmouth traffic, culminating in 1858 with the 'Battle of Havant': at the opening of the

Above left:
The IWR's 2-4-0Ts were small but not weaklings. This one is forging up the demanding Apse Bank on the long climb from Sandown to Ventnor with a sizeable train of four-wheelers. *IAL/Bucknall Coll*

Left:
Extract from the 1974 summer timetable (Saturday service 25 May to 7 September).

Above:
Built and owned jointly by the LBSC & LSWR, the St Johns Road to Pier Head line was operated by the island companies. An IWCR train is seen leaving Pier Head behind No 4. *IAL/Bucknall Coll*

LSWR's Portsmouth direct line from London, which joined the longer, rival LBSCR route at Havant, large gangs of railway navvies from the two sides faced each other for a major brawl and a locomotive was chained to the rails across the junction. By the 1870s the companies had put such crude methods of competition behind them and in fact co-operated to improve the cross-Solent trade. The high-level line from Portsmouth & Southsea station to Portsmouth Harbour, where the station was extended out on a short pier to a landing stage, was a joint exercise. Across the Solent, they built a third pier alongside the original and the tramway ones, to carry a double-track railway the half-mile out to sea. At the pierhead a three-platform terminus was built, while land was reclaimed on the beach to make room for Ryde Esplanade station and the ramp down to Esplanade Tunnel. The double track plunged down at 1 in 50 to below high tide level, then swung

under the eastern edge of the town to emerge near the tramway route north of St Johns Road station, where an end-on junction was made with the IWR and IWCR lines.

Having ensured at last that the journey to the island's fast-growing resorts was as convenient as possible, the LSWR and LBSCR handed their line over to the IWR and IWCR to operate with their own stock. The land section of the horse tramway closed and the railways of Ryde took on the basic form they have kept to this day.

By the turn of the century, two ventures with far less potential had been completed elsewhere on the island. These were a line from Newport to the far west of the island and one from Merstone on the Newport Junction line to Ventnor. Why anyone thought Ventnor needed two different railway routes, especially as this new one passed through nowhere of any consequence, is hard to imagine. But the Newport, Godshill & St Lawrence Railway was slowly and thriftily built, reaching St Lawrence in 1897 and a new station on the western fringe of Ventnor in 1900. With a fine cheek that these days would fall foul of trading standards laws, the new station was named Ventnor Town, which fooled nobody — at any rate not after their first journey! The branch soon settled down to a sparse service, for which a single-coach rail-motor and later a pair of four-wheel coaches operated push-pull was adequate, for half a century until BR closed it in 1952, at a time in which a railway still had to be a *really* hopeless case to be closed.

The other line, the independent Freshwater, Yarmouth & Newport, rambled across the northern plain of West Wight, passing no settlements of any size apart from those in its name. Yarmouth,

almost 10 miles from Newport, was a small coastal village linked to the mainland by a ferry and already being mentioned in rumours about plans for a Solent Tunnel — rumours which have persisted, on and off, to the present day. The FYNR then ran alongside the River Yar to Freshwater, where it expired, rather than terminated, on the very edge of West Wight's only significant town, as if too tired, and certainly too broke, to go any further. A mile to the west was the bay and small resort of Totland and a mile to the south was

Freshwater Bay, both of which could have found better railway connections to Ryde mutually beneficial, but it was not to be. The FYNR remained in control but impoverished until the Grouping, by when it was too late to think of extensions.

Small and poor the FYNR might have been but it was fiercely independent. Like the IW(NJ)R, it did not at first please the Railway Inspectorate, who made several visits before they were satisfied that the line had been brought up to a standard that was safe for the travelling public. The big concern

had been that the formation and civil engineering might fall to bits under the strain of passing trains! The line was originally operated by the IWCR but the FYNR fell out with that company in 1913 in a row over charges. After months of wrangling, things got to the point where in effect the IWCR told the FYNR that if it was not satisfied it could run its own trains and the FYNR replied that all right it would, so there. It then had to face the interesting logistical problem of acquiring locomotives and rolling stock to do so without the funds to buy them. The story of its purchases is told later but it did produce the interesting paradox that the most struggling of the island's pre-Grouping railways owned the most modern steam engine to operate on Wight until the 1970s.

This was not the only problem the FYNR had caused for itself. At Newport its junction with the IWCR was north of the station and faced north, so its trains had the inconvenience of running into a headshunt and then reversing into the platforms, and vice versa for Freshwater-bound trains. The IWCR withdrew this facility after the 1913 dispute, and the FYNR had to build in great haste a basic platform and runround loop on what had been its approach curve to Newport station. Passengers were now faced with a short but unwelcome walk between the two stations. Happily the IWCR relented before long but the disused halt remained for years, the fossilised relic of a dispute.

The FYNR was also one of the last companies to be amalgamated in the Grouping. It was not absorbed by the Southern Railway until September 1923, and then under duress, at the orders of the Amalgamation Tribunal. The FYNR had an inflated idea of its own financial worth, based on the upsurge in traffic that the Solent Tunnel would bring: bait that the Southern Railway prudently but unsportingly refused to bite!

The FYNR apart, the island's railways were all part of the Southern Railway by early 1923 and the era of the biggest investment in the system's history began. New locomotives, new coaches, new wagons; well, new to the island, and although it was all second-hand, it was still much more recent than the existing relics, many of which had passed their half-century of service. Track and signalling was improved, Smallbrook finally became a genuine junction, with double track north from there to Pier Head (in the summer months, that is; in winter the signalbox was shut and the lines reverted to being parallel single lines from St Johns Road) and Brading to Sandown was doubled. All this was intended to help the system cope properly with its heavy summer traffic, especially the massive arrival and departure flows

Left:
The IWCR's Beyer Peacocks were smaller than their contemporaries on the IWR. No 4 approaches Sandown with a train from Newport. No two coaches in the train match.
IAL/Bucknall Coll

Below left:
Due to its 1913 dispute with the IWCR, the Freshwater, Yarmouth & Newport Railway had to provide itself with engines, coaches and a Newport station in a tearing hurry. FYN No 2, the 'Terrier' bought third-hand from the South Western and still in LSWR livery and with the Drummond boiler it carried for years, is seen with the FYN's seven ex-Great Central coaches at Newport station. The runround loop shows signs of recent and hasty construction. *LPC*

Above right:
A new sense of order and purpose followed the Southern Railway takeover in 1923. This view (1924 or 1925) of No 22 *Brading* leaving Sandown for Ventnor shows a remarkably uniform train compared with earlier pictures; all nine ex-North London Railway coaches have apparently been formed into a set. No 22 arrived on the island in mid-1924. *LPC*

Right:
Extract from the BR 1957-8 winter timetable (weekday service).

on Saturdays; but for nine months of the year it all reverted to being a peaceful rural system. Too peaceful, and in all honesty too lavish. On the eastern half of the island there was scarcely any point more than two miles from a railway, a network density equalled nowhere outside the mainland's major cities. But on the island, apart from the east coast line, Cowes and Newport, there were no towns near the railways.

These interwar years were the system's zenith, however, and the prosperous summers compensated for the lean months out of season. The system had a semi-autonomous status within the SR; in charge was the Isle of Wight Assistant, who reported to the General Manager. In practice he was the GM of this isolated piece of the network. The most notable holder of the office was Alistair B. MacLeod, one of the great enthusiastic railwaymen of the middle of the century. His regime, from 1928 to 1936, saw many improvements which revitalised the island's

railways.

The SR years were the ones which saw the 'O2s' arrive. These comparatively small 0-4-4 tank engines, which came to dominate the system and for nearly a decade were the exclusive motive power, first appeared on the island as soon after the Grouping as a pair could be got ready and shipped across, so urgent was the need for new locomotives. Additions followed steadily through the next 15 years, with older island locos being withdrawn as fast as 'O2s' could be released by the SR to replace them. These engines came to symbolise the Isle of Wight lines to enthusiasts and at their peak in the early 1950s there were 23 of them there, almost all shedded at Ryde.

A similar revolution was taking place with coaching stock, where several phases of replacement, and then replacement of the replacements, took the system from running a very mixed bag including some real relics to almost total dominance by a fleet of ex-London, Chatham &

¶ Portsmouth Harbour .. dep	..	..	..	..	1135		..	..	Arr Rowlands Castle 11 56 am Saturdays only	Mondays to Fridays Arr Rowlands Castle 11 56 am	..	1235		Arr Rowlands Castle 12 26 pm	..	..	..	..	1 35		..	..	..	..	..	2 35		..	..	..	..	..	..	..
‖ Ryde Pier Head .... arr	..	..	..	..	12 5		..	..			..	1 5			..	..	..	..	2 5		..	..	..	..	..	3 5		..	..	..	..	..	..	..
Ryde, Pier Head § .. dep	..	..	..	..	1218	1225	..	..			..	1 18	1 25		..	..	..	..	2 18	2 25	..	..	..	..	..	3 18	3 25	..	..	..	..	..	..	..
" Esplanade §	..	..	..	..	1220	1228	..	..			..	1 20	1 28		..	..	..	..	2 20	2 28	..	..	..	..	..	3 20	3 28	..	..	..	..	..	..	..
" St. John's Road	..	..	..	..	1224	1232	..	..			..	1 24	1 32		..	..	..	..	2 24	2 32	..	..	..	..	..	3 24	3 32	..	..	..	..	..	..	..
Brading	..	..	..	..	..	1240	..	..			..	..	1 40		..	..	..	..	..	2 40	..	..	..	..	..	..	3 40	..	..	..	..	..	..	..
Sandown	..	..	..	..	..	1245	..	..			..	..	1 45		..	..	..	..	..	2 45	..	..	..	..	..	..	3 45	..	..	..	..	..	..	..
Shanklin	..	..	..	..	..	1254	..	..			..	..	1 54		..	..	..	..	..	2 54	..	..	..	..	..	..	3 54	..	..	..	..	..	..	..
Wroxall	..	..	..	..	..	1 4	..	..			..	..	2 4		..	..	..	..	..	3 4	..	..	..	..	..	..	4 4	..	..	..	..	..	..	..
Ventnor .... arr	..	..	..	..	..	1 10	..	..			..	..	2 10		..	..	..	..	..	3 10	..	..	..	..	..	..	4 10	..	..	..	..	..	..	..
Ashey .. .. dep	..	..	..	..	1231	..	..	..			..	1 31	..	..	..	..	..	..	2 31	..	..	..	..	..	..	3 31	..	..	..	..	..	..	..	..
Haven Street	..	..	..	..	1235	..	..	..			..	1 35	..	..	..	..	..	..	2 35	..	..	..	..	..	..	3 35	..	..	..	..	..	..	..	..
Newport .. .. .. arr	..	..	..	..	1245	..	..	..			..	1 45	..	..	..	..	..	..	2 45	..	..	..	..	..	..	3 45	..	..	..	..	..	..	..	..
Newport dep	..	..	..	..	1247	..	..	..			..	1 47	..	..	..	..	..	..	2 47	..	..	..	..	..	..	3 47	..	..	..	..	..	..	..	..
Mill Hill	..	..	..	..	1257	..	..	..			..	1 57	..	..	..	..	..	..	2 57	..	..	..	..	..	..	3 57	..	..	..	..	..	..	..	..
Cowes .... arr	..	..	..	..	1259	..	..	..			..	1 59	..	..	..	..	..	..	2 59	..	..	..	..	..	..	3 59	..	..	..	..	..	..	..	..

Dover and ex-LBSCR bogie coaches with reasonably up to date standards of passenger comfort.

After World War 2 things at first returned much to normal, at least so far as the tourist traffic was concerned. But the byway lines had run out of time. The Ventnor West branch (the SR had renamed the station) went first, in 1952, followed the next year by the Bembridge and Freshwater lines, and then Newport-Sandown in 1956. This left Ryde-Ventnor and Ryde-Newport-Cowes, the fairly busy rump of the system. Indeed, the closure of the Ventnor line in particular would have been catastrophic to the island's economy at that time. A replacement bus service for moving the tourists would have required, it was estimated, 100 buses. They would have brought the east coast roads to a standstill, alienated everyone and driven the tourists away.

This is not to say that this first round of closures was well received. Cars were still the possessions of a minority and anyway, use them or not, people liked to feel that the railways were available. As a price for accepting the closures the island Council extracted an undertaking from BR that the Cowes line would not be closed without five years' notice, and seven years' notice would be given for the Ventnor line. In time the Council was to learn the hard way precisely what a British Railways undertaking was worth.

On the surviving lines things continued much as before, although the goods traffic was fading away, and it sometimes seemed that it would go on for ever. The engines, all ex-LSWR 'O2s' by now, were painted lined black and the pre-Grouping bogie coaches were in Southern Region green, but otherwise the scene seemed timeless. Beneath the surface all was not so well. Few of the coaches and none of the locomotives were less than 50 years old and all had seen plenty of service before being shipped to the island. Quite simply, the stock was wearing out. It was said in 1963 that no engine was left without a cracked mainframe, bogie frames

Left:
Immaculate in SR Maunsell livery at Newport in 1931, No 29 *Alverstone* shows the typical features of an early-period island 'O2': Drummond boiler, bell-whistle and original bunker with coal-rails. *LPC*

Below left:
The IWR's locos remained in SR service for some years. No W16 *Wroxall* pilots an unidentified 'O2' out of St Johns Road on a long train of ex-LCDR four-wheel stock in the summer of 1931; another 'O2' passes northbound, its leading coach being an ex-LSWR bogie. Both trains are probably Ventnor services. *Wroxall* was withdrawn in June 1933. *IAL*

Right:
The energetic and innovative Island Manager A. B. MacLeod (right), outside Ryde Works with two of his senior staff in 1930. With bowler hat, umbrella and briefcase, ABM was clearly 'upper-middle management'. (Contemporary pictures of SR senior officers and directors show serried ranks of top hats.) *IAL*

were wearing beyond repair and that Westinghouse brake pumps were being cased in sheet steel as the only way left to stop them squirting passing passengers with hot water.

All could have been put right, but at huge cost and the sort of effort now associated with preservation's major restorations. Alternatively, the lines could be re-equipped — or closed. But something had to be done, and as the winter traffic was declining and even the tourist trade was showing signs of decay, there was less financial incentive to do it.

There were also the island's own peculiar problems. The lines had never been upgraded as mainland branches had been, so the axleload limit was tight. Modern coaching stock was simply too large for the antiquated loading gauge and too long for some of the curves; the centre throw-over would catch lineside structures. The last coaches to arrive, ex-SECR ones to replace the LCDR stock in the late 1940s, had needed some surgery to squeeze into the island's loading gauge, and anything now available on BR would need little short of a total rebuild: that, or some hugely expensive civil engineering on the island.

Serious thought was given in the late 1950s to replacing the 'O2s' with Ivatt Class 2 tanks. Mainland trials began but were suspended when

BR came up with a more radical plan. It seems that the decision was made secretly in 1962 to abandon the system after the 1964 holiday season. Only the Ryde Pier section would remain, linking the ferry to a new bus station next to Esplanade station. At that stage, ex-London Underground stock fitted with diesel engines appears to have been the favoured stock option for a pier shuttle service.

Disquiet about the railway's future had been growing for some time and an IoW Railways Retention Association now existed. Part at least of the BR plan was leaked to it and in early January 1963 the Association announced that BR intended to close the island lines in September 1964. BR promptly denied it as 'rubbish' and the Association was attacked as foolish and irresponsible by the Island Council and the island's MP, both Council and MP quoting faithfully BR's five/seven years' undertaking.

The bombshell, when it came in late February 1963, was devastating. BR announced that the system was to close, apart from Pier Head to Esplanade, in October 1964. The Association, vindicated, rubbed a few official noses in it. Council and MP reacted with fury, declaring themselves tricked, cheated and betrayed. The MP threatened to resign the Government whip. Out of

Above left:
Smallbrook Junction, with the signalman holding out the single line token to Brading. Creation of the junction to improve summer services was one of the SR's many improvements to the island system.
Andrew Muckley

Left:
Another SR innovation was the transfer to the island of four 'E1' 0-6-0Ts to take charge of the heavier goods workings. No W2 *Yarmouth* is seen nearing Newport with a coal train from Medina Wharf in May 1933.
H. C. Casserley

Above:
Nationalisation in 1948 is marked on No 34 *Newport* by painting 'British Railways' in SR-style 'sunshine' lettering on the malachite green livery, pending a decision on new national liveries. The result looked good — a pity it was not retained! *F. W. Day*

the furore came the compromise of retention and electrification of Ryde to Shanklin only, which cynics suggested was what BR had wanted all along but would not have got had it not proposed something more drastic and appeared to give concessions.

An extra year was also won but in early 1966 the reduction and modernisation of the Isle of Wight lines got under way. Ryde Pier had already been rebuilt and strengthened in recent winters. Next, the closures took place. Smallbrook to Cowes closed on 21 February 1966, followed by Shanklin-Ventnor on 18 April. The absurdity of closing that section before, rather than after, the tourist season served to increase the bitterness that this closure aroused.[1] Ventnor, it was claimed, would be crippled by the loss of the railway, and its tourist trade would not survive the loss. This proved to be largely true.

The official reason given for closure of Shanklin-Ventnor was that it was seriously unprofitable but two other probable reasons have since emerged from people who were in BR middle management at the time. One was that to electrify to Ventnor would have required an additional electric sub-station, to which the budget would not stretch. The other was that BR's hidden agenda was for complete closure in a few years, by which time traffic would have dwindled sufficiently for there to be little fuss about it. This has proved to have been a serious miscalculation.

The much reduced steam operation continued through that last year while preparation work went on around it. Even so, a peak Saturday required 10

[1] *To be fair, both these sections were originally due to close in late 1965 but the non-availability of buses as replacement led to a postponement.*

engines in steam, often burning some pretty frightful coal that was being swept up and despatched to Ryde by closing steam MPDs around the Southern Region.

At the end of December the final trains ran and the system was closed for several months while preparations for electrification reached a peak. Heavy rationalisation was the order of the day and goods facilities were withdrawn. The Works and MPD at St Johns Road were reduced to a new facility in the former carriage repair shop, most sidings were lifted and there were considerable staff redundancies. Remaining steam stock was worked over the disused line to Newport, where it was stored pending scrapping. It was at this stage that new players in the field appeared — preservationists. Their story, which has been increasingly entwined with the BR line, is told later.

For operating the line, elderly EMUs were bought from London Underground. Nearly as old as some of the steam-hauled stock they were replacing, this withdrawn tube stock was to spend over 20 years in increasingly geriatric service on the island, while to keep it running, Ryde Works staff performed miracles that at least matched their efforts on the steam stock in former years.

The stock was adapted for three-rail running and given extra luggage space by removing some seats. At stations tracks were raised (or platforms lowered) and the reduction in overall height of the running fleet meant that the rail level in Esplanade Tunnel could be raised, with a big reduction in the

Left:
Working bunker-first from Ryde, No 20 *Shanklin* nears Sandown with a Ventnor train on 11 June 1952. The first four coaches of the set are ex-LBSCR.
Brian Morrison

Below left:
Cowes station shows signs of life in both up and down sidings as 'E1' No 3 *Ryde* waits to depart with a Railway Correspondence & Travel Society special on 18 May 1952. The loco still bears 'British Railways' in full on its side tanks. *E. D. Bruton*

Below:
Regular double-heading on the island was unusual; ironically, in later years it was most often seen on one of the lightest trains! The summer Saturdays 07.50 Ryde-Ventnor parcels train, sometimes only one or two vans strong, as seen here in July 1965, took a pilot engine to Sandown, where it commenced its solo duties on an up passenger working that commenced there. No 24 *Calbourne*, with its nameplates removed, leads No 29 *Alverstone* near Smallbrook Junction.
A. E. Bennett

number of times that it needed pumping out after flooding by extra-high tides.

Old it may have been but the electric stock had been spruced up nicely and it was well received by residents and visitors alike. Coupled with the raising of the speed limit from 40 to 45mph and a more frequent off-peak service, it gave a new sense of modernity to the surviving line that did much to improve its image with the public.

By the late 1980s passenger traffic, though it had fallen, had not collapsed and the attitude towards rail closures had so changed that the surviving line's future was fairly secure. However, it was clearly overdue for another rehabilitation. Even the ordinary passenger, bouncing along in increasingly latchety old tube stock, could not fail to notice that things were getting a little distressed! By now Network SouthEast was at its peak and resources were found. The service had settled down to a basic 20min frequency and the line was rebuilt around this. Three trains were needed for this service, passing at or just north of Sandown and at or just south of St Johns Road. To reduce maintenance costs, Brading-Sandown was singled, with an automated passing loop at Sandown, which became the fixed, regular crossing place, and control of the line was centralised in St Johns Road signalbox. Ryde Works was modernised and in 1989 another batch of second-hand tube stock was drafted in.

This time it was ex-1938 stock and was given a much more thorough overhaul and face-lift before arrival than the 1924 stock had received. Arranged to run in two-car sets for multiple-unit operation,

Left:
The Ryde Pier section, almost unique to the Isle of Wight system, was part of what made it all so fascinating to enthusiasts. On 17 April 1965 No 16 *Ventnor* departs with the 17.25 to Ventnor, while another 'O2' waits alongside. No 16 carries its number, Southern-style, on its front buffer beam; a lack of smokebox door numberplates was one of the island system's little quirks of semi-autonomy. Pier Head signalbox seemed almost to hover over the water — not a posting for the over-imaginative. *M. York*

Centre left:
St Johns Road on 16 September 1963. No 22 *Brading* runs in with a Pier Head to Ventnor service while No 14 *Fishbourne* has arrived with the Ventnor-St Johns Road freight and waits to shunt it into the yard. 'O2s' took over full responsibility for freight traffic after the demise of the 'E1s'. The shield round the Westinghouse pump is to protect passing passengers from a hot shower! *P. Paye*

Below:
Newport after closure in 1966. Demolition work has started as an 'O2' heads an engineering train of electrification materials past wagonloads of coal and through the station. *T. R. Genower*

the new trains looked surprisingly smart and gave quite an up to date impression. A new station had already been opened at Lake, between Sandown and Shanklin; it was now joined by the first ever station at Smallbrook, an interchange between the NSE line and the newly extended preserved line, the Isle of Wight Steam Railway. Happily, it was named Smallbrook Junction, not Smallbrook Interchange, and although there is no physical connection between the two systems, the possibility has never been ruled out.

Inevitably, the next momentous event to hit the railway was privatisation, though the authorities did at least have the sense to dispose of it as an integrated, self-contained package, rather than leaving Railtrack responsible for an isolated piece of empire. The Isle of Wight Railway's long tradition of semi-autonomy was not destroyed.

After a surprisingly protracted bidding process, during which it looked at one stage as if a consortium of the local authority, the ferry company, the preserved railway and other bodies might be successful, the line went in due course to Stagecoach. There has so far been no major upheaval and in fact encouraging noises about co-operation are being made. It remains to be seen how the future of this remarkable survivor of a railway will develop in the years to come.

Below:
In September 1966, with the pier lines closed for major rebuilding, an up Shanklin train leaves St Johns Road to terminate at Esplanade. With no runround facilities, an engine is attached at the rear to head the down working. No 17 *Seaview* heads the train, with No 16 *Ventnor* bringing up the rear. *R. H. Tunstall*

Left:
Evening of steam in more ways than one, as No 17 *Seaview* waits at Ryde Esplanade with the 17.25 to Shanklin on 30 December 1966, the last day but one of Isle of Wight steam. *Brian Stephenson*

Left:
In February 1989 two first-generation island electric units pass at Sandown. Both carry Network SouthEast livery and the local 'RydeRail' marketing brand name. Behind them, Sandown signalbox looks incongruously tall without the surrounding platform canopy, above which it once reared.
Mike Jones

Left:
The new order; newly refurbished ex-LT 1938 stock as NSE unit No 483001, waits to leave Pier Head on its official inaugural run to Brading on 13 July 1989. *Brian Morrison*

Locomotives

The locomotive history of the island's railways divides neatly into two, with a short postscript. The main division is, as with so much else, the Grouping of 1923.

While it would be unjust to call the pre-1923 position haphazard, or even unplanned, there was a sense of order and purpose apparent after 1923, which came from a larger organisation, with resources to spare and invest, being in charge. Before then, though locomotive policies certainly existed, they were often constrained by the budget. Indeed, things were so tight at one time that some of the directors of the IWCR set up an independent company to run a hire-purchase scheme for that railway to buy locomotives — a dedicated finance house, in fact. How that would square with modern company law is unclear but at the time it served to get the IWCR out of a tight corner.

The island's locomotive history is dominated by four types, three of them being 'imported' classes. The fourth, and chronologically the first, Beyer Peacock 2-4-0Ts, is almost our starting point.

But first of all were the early engines of the Cowes & Newport and it is here that our review must start.

The C&N's First Engines

The Cowes & Newport began its career with a pair of 2-2-2 outside-cylinder well-tank engines. They were purchased new from Slaughter Gruning and were typical products of their time. Unluckily for them, they were designed and built on the eve of

Below:
Maker's photograph of C&N No 1 *Pioneer* as built. *IAL*

Above:
Pictured near the end of its life, No 1 shows the many changes made over some 40 years, not least being the loss of its name. *IAL*

one of the great leaps forward in design that feature in British locomotive history. Within 15 years they were clearly outmoded and outclassed. They were also underpowered for most of the system. That said, they managed a respectable working life of nearly 40 years, lasting until withdrawal in Edwardian days.

Named *Pioneer* and *Precursor*, these little tanks did not at first carry numbers. They became Nos 1 and 2 as the fleet expanded. The basic features of the design would have been familiar on many mid-Victorian minor and branch lines. Driving wheels of 5ft 3in and a boiler pressure of 120psi gave a tractive effort of 4,720lb and they weighed 19 tons 5cwt in working order.

Adequate for the Cowes-Newport service, they found the extended line to Ryde rather beyond their powers. Their later years were spent largely on the Newport-Freshwater line, somewhat to the disgust of the FYNR's directors; having been told that the IWCR needed to buy extra stock to operate their line, they had rather expected to see these new arrivals on their services, rather than the main route's outmoded cast-offs. It was one of the bones of contention that were to build up into the row of 1913.

The pair had sole charge of C&N trains until 1870, when they were joined by *Mill Hill*, a Black Hawthorn 0-4-2T. A small industrial machine, *Mill Hill's* 3ft 3in driving wheels gave it a tractive effort

of 5,190lb — and a very limited turn of speed! Unsurprisingly, it was purchased with the role of standby engine in mind; it spent its later career as the regular Medina Wharf shunter.

The Beyer Peacock 2-4-0Ts

Close on the heels of the C&N came the IWR and its Ryde-Shanklin line, for which it bought the first of what became the typical pre-Grouping Isle of Wight locomotive, the Beyer Peacocks. They were to become the mainstay of the Ryde-Ventnor line and the IWCR ordered some too for its own routes. They cannot strictly be called a class as they varied in size, the later IWR engines being larger and those of the Central were noticeably smaller. But they were obviously all of the same family. [1]

[1] *The island's 2-4-0Ts make one of the curious points of parallel and comparison between the island's railways and the Isle of Man Railway, which also had a penchant for Beyer Peacock 2-4-0Ts, though of a somewhat smaller size and with outside cylinders.*

Right:
A 19th-century portrait of IWR
Beyer Peacock *Sandown* (no IWR
loco carried a number), after the
cab had been fitted but with original
chimney and boiler, dome over the
firebox and high side handrails.
Various shed staff have hastened to
join the footplate crew for this
formal photograph. *LPC*

Below:
IWR *Ventnor* in later condition, with
new boiler, locally cast chimney,
simpler dome with Salter valves
sitting parallel rather than splayed,
extra safety valve on the firebox
and, of course, Westinghouse
brakes. *LPC*

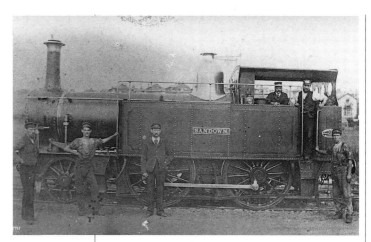

The first of the type were the first three delivered to the IWR in June 1864, in good time for the line's opening on 23 August. *Ryde*, *Sandown* and *Shanklin* were initially part of an order for five engines, which was cut back to three when the IWR had a second look at its budget. Robust products, as would be expected from Beyer Peacock, they had that builder's typical features of the era. They all lasted through various rebuilds to the Grouping; *Sandown* was the first to go, being withdrawn with a cracked frame in 1923, after 49 years' service; *Ryde* lasted until 1932.

Cylinders of 15in by 20in, 5ft driving wheels and 120psi boiler pressure gave a tractive effort of 7,650lb. That gave them the ability to cope with the demands of the service but three engines were not sufficient motive power as the line's business began to pick up, particularly the summer tourist trade and especially once the line was completed to Ventnor.

As a stopgap, a small 2-4-0T that had worked for the line's constructors was purchased in 1867. Named *Brading*, it was part of the fleet for less than five years, being displaced by further Beyer Peacocks as the IWR's finances improved.

The fourth Beyer Peacock, *Ventnor*, in fact arrived the following year, 1868, and was basically the same as its older sisters. It was followed by

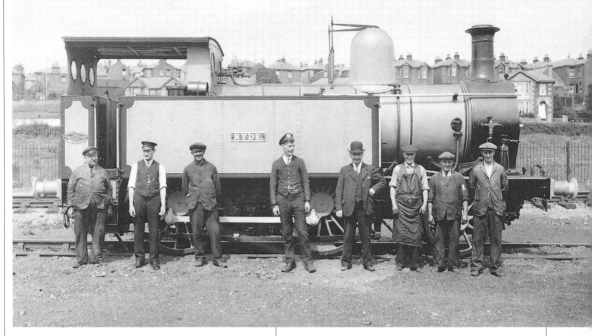

Three aspects of *Ryde*

Above left:
Ryde at Ventnor in Edwardian days, with new boiler but still carrying its original chimney, bell-mouth dome cover and high handrails. *IAL/Bucknall Coll*

Left:
No W13 *Ryde* at Newport circa 1930, carrying its name again and looking smart in SR livery. Chimney and dome cover have been changed and the loco . now carries a 'hooter' whistle in common with most of the fleet. *IAL*

Above:
After withdrawal, *Ryde* was given a cosmetic overhaul at St Johns Road, restoring some of its earlier features, before dispatch to Eastleigh for storage pending planned exhibition in a museum. The works team, with Foreman A. Brading, pose with the loco on completion of the job. Sadly the wartime scrap drive was to claim *Ryde*. *A. B. MacLeod/IAL*

Wroxall in 1872, the same apart from marginally larger wheels, a result of developments in tyre manufacture, which slightly reduced its nominal tractive effort — at least until the tyres were turned down.

The final two, *Brading* and *Bonchurch*, arrived in 1876 and 1883 respectively. They were larger than their predecessors, *Bonchurch* being the larger of

the two, with bigger boilers, cylinders and fuel capacity, though boiler pressure remained the same, 120psi being rather low by the 1880s. Tractive efforts were 10,360lb (*Brading*) and 11,700lb (*Bonchurch*).

Bonchurch was a more modern machine in various ways, having, for instance, Ramsbottom safety valves and a plain dome. It also had the dubious distinction of falling off its delivery barge into the sea while being delivered to St Helens in bad weather. It had to spend a week on the seabed until the gale blew itself out, after which it was salvaged and completed its journey to Ryde Works on its own wheels. Despite its experiences, it was in traffic within a month. The most powerful engine in the IWR fleet, it was claimed to be the strongest on the island system. Certainly, after the Grouping it could hold its own with the nominally much more powerful 'O2s' on the summer Ryde-Ventnor services.

The locomotives evolved as they went through rebuilds over the years, significant changes being the reboilerings around the turn of the century, which saw the domes and Salter valves move forward on the earlier machines, and the fitting of new cylinder blocks as required at around the same time. From the crews' view, two more controversial changes were the fitting of cabs in place of primitive weather-boards, and the installation of full, automatic brakes. Both these developments led to protests (on the grounds that they inhibited the crews from doing their jobs properly) but soon became accepted.

Meanwhile the Central had also bought some of the type, doubtless influenced by the IWR's purchases. The first were ordered by the Ryde & Newport before it opened in 1875. It was obvious that the combined C&N and R&N services would need more motive power but Beyer Peacock was in fact the second choice, after an incident which can have done the line's engineer's reputation no favours. The R&N bought a pair of second-hand 2-4-0Ts from the LSWR on his say-so, and it was not realised until they arrived at Southampton for shipping across that their outside cylinders made them foul of the R&N's loading gauge. The sale had to be cancelled in haste, which doubtless caused LSWR officers irritation and amusement in equal measure!

From this little disaster recourse was had to Beyer Peacock, and a pair of 2-4-0Ts was ordered, arriving in mid-1876. Named *Cowes* and *Osborne*, they were numbered 4 and 5 after the formation of the IWCR in 1887. They relieved the R&N's two stop-gap locos, *Dorothy*, which is believed to have been the IWR's first *Brading* in yet another incarnation, and the contractor's loco *Bee* which had helped build the line.

Noticeably smaller than the IWR's engines, *Cowes* and *Osborne* had a tractive effort of 6,660lb. They were bought from the makers by hire-purchase, payment being spread over five years — an ominous sign for the future.

The Joint Committee and later the IWCR then made a series of one-off purchases over the years, second-hand or new. In 1889 the third Beyer Peacock 2-4-0T arrived, No 8. Slightly larger than Nos 4 and 5, it had a boiler pressure of 150psi, raising its tractive effort to 8,200lb.

The last of the type was bought second-hand from the Midland & South Western Junction Railway. Originally built in 1882, it arrived on the Central in 1906. Given No 7 (replacing an earlier No 7 which was scrapped), it was the largest of the Central's series and had a tractive effort of 9,500lb. In size it was similar to the IWR's engines.

The Beyer Peacocks were to dominate the island railways for some 60 years and the final withdrawals were not until the early 1930s. One of the last to go, *Ryde*, was by then clearly a relic, as the oldest locomotive in use on the Southern Railway. Thanks to the efforts of A. B. MacLeod, it was set aside for preservation, given a cosmetic overhaul and reinstatement of some original fittings at Ryde Works, and sent to Eastleigh for storage, along with a few other historic machines which were being retained for a planned museum. Unfortunately for them the World War 2 'scrap drive' was deemed more important and they were cut up.

Below left:
An early view of one of the IWC's Beyer Peacocks;
Osborne is seen in R&N condition, named and un-
numbered and with very high handrails to facilitate a
journey along the top of the tanks. It became IWC
No 5, keeping this under the Southern, and was
withdrawn in 1926. *IAL*

Above:
IWC No 4, probably in the 1900s, carrying the
company's title in full on the lined metallic red livery.
IAL/Bucknall Coll

Other Pre-Grouping Locomotives

Apart from its Beyer Peacocks, the IWR had only
one other member of the fleet for any significant
time. This was a Manning Wardle 'M' class
0-6-0ST, one of that company's standard series of
industrial saddle tanks.

Named *Bembridge*, the engine was largely
associated with the Brading-Bembridge branch,
which it worked from opening in 1882, although it
remained the property of the Brading Harbour &
Railway Co until sold to the IWR in 1898. A
tractive effort of 8,620lb and 22½ tons of adhesive
weight made it ideal for the sidings at St Helens as
well as the branch passenger service.

In 1916 *Bembridge* left the island for military
service following a government request to
purchase surplus engines. One feels in retrospect
that the IWR was following the old Russian

practice of shooting one horse for the wolves so
that you could escape with the rest! As the non-
standard member of the fleet it could most readily
be spared. *Bembridge* spent its military career on
the army railways of Wiltshire and Hampshire,
before being scrapped in about 1920.

The Central by contrast developed a much more
varied fleet, not so much by planning as a case of
'needs must'. First purchase after Nos 4 and 5 was
forced on the Joint Committee following its
assumption of management of the Newport
Junction line. Recently completed and opened
throughout after its protracted gestation, this line
had depended on two 2-2-2Ts; *Comet*, on hire
from the LSWR (and returned in 1875) and
Newport, which had actually been purchased by
the company chairman. Numbered 6 by the Joint
Committee, it was a sickly machine, finally
withdrawn in 1890 after a career notable chiefly for
the frequency of its failures in traffic. With the extra
mileage now being operated forcing the
Committee to look for something more reliable, it
cast around on the second-hand market,
eventually being offered a 4-4-0T by the North
London Railway.

As No 7 *Whippingham*, the new recruit was by
far the most powerful engine in the growing fleet,
with a tractive effort of 9,700lb. Another Slaughter
Gruning machine, it was already 19 years old on
arrival but even so was something of a bargain at
£750 — the Committee had been prepared to pay
up to £1,000 but other mainland companies

Above left:
In the post-World War 1 years, IWC No 5 drifts into St Johns Road carrying black livery with 'IWC' lettering just visible on the side tank. *IAL/Bucknall Coll*

Left:
The IWC's second No 7, the largest of its Beyer Peacocks, joined the fleet in 1908. *IAL/Bucknall Coll*

Above:
Maker's photograph of IWC No 8, built in 1898. Noticeably smaller than No 7, it carries the 'garter' livery, the lettering around the number reading simply 'Central Railway'. *IAL*

Above right:
No 8 shows well the IWC's final livery of lined black with the shaded 'I.W.C.' on the sides. *IAL/Bucknall Coll*

Right:
SR No W8 at Newport in the mid 1920s, showing few changes from original condition. It was withdrawn in 1929. *LPC*

approached had had nothing suitable in that price bracket. *Whippingham* spent much of its career on the Newport-Sandown service, on which the Committee pinned hopes of growing prosperity, linking as it did the eastern holiday resorts with the Cowes ferry. Designed by William Adams (the first of many of his engines to work on the island, as it turned out), *Whippingham* lasted until 1902, after a respectable life of 42 hard-working years.

The Joint Committee companies amalgamated into the Isle of Wight Central in 1887 and two years later, having agreed to operate the FYNR's services, was shopping around again, for a loco to meet this additional commitment. The second-hand market proved fruitless, so a rather fine new 4-4-0T was ordered from Black Hawthorn. Bigger and more powerful than anything else in the fleet, with a tractive effort of 11,600lb, it was given No 6 in place of the recently withdrawn *Newport*. This was the loco that the FYN directors were disappointed not to get pulling their trains!

The Central's little empire had not yet reached its full extent, for the Newport, Godshill & St Lawrence was to land on its lap. Incorporated in 1889, it took eight years to open to St Lawrence and another three to complete to Ventnor in 1900. Again, it increased the Central's need for motive power, hence the arrival of Beyer Peacock No 8 in 1898 and the first 'Terrier', followed by three more to replace the withdrawn Nos 1 and 2. The next 'one-off' purchase however, in 1906, was a railmotor, a small locomotive and short coach combined, with the power unit forming one end and one bogie of the coach. The concept enjoyed a brief popularity on Edwardian railways before the disadvantages became too evident and the Central

Above:
The IWR's 'odd man out', Manning Wardle *Bembridge*, seen in the yard at St Johns Road. *IAL/Bucknall Coll*

Above right:
The IWC's original No 7 was this ex-North London Railway 4-4-0T. Arriving on the IWC in 1880, it was scrapped in 1906. *IAL/Bucknall Coll*

Below right:
Ordered new from Black Hawthorn in 1890, this 4-4-0T took IWC No 6 in place of the recently withdrawn little *Newport*. Seen here in rather tired condition at Newport shortly before the Grouping (the letters 'I.W.' can just be discerned on the original print), the loco lasted until 1925. *IAL*

could be accused of jumping on a bandwagon. Like other lines, it was to regret it after a first flush of enthusiasm. First, however, impressed by the economy of its new unit, the Central wanted another and hit on the cheap option of encasing little 0-4-2T No 3 and buying a coach for it to work with. Bizarrely, it chose a clerestory-roofed composite on six-wheel bogies from the Midland Railway. The coach had a long career, though heavily rebuilt on the island, but its railmotor career was fairly short — the assembly was too slow and cumbersome to find favour for long. The sprightlier No 1 lasted only until 1910, though the coach portion, with a normal bogie added at the former engine end, returned to traffic.

With No 7 well and truly worn out, it was replaced by second-hand Beyer Peacock No 7 in 1906. The next purchase was the last the Central

made, and this time it made a bad bargain. The new No 2 arrived in mid-1909; built in 1895 for the Marquis of Londonderry's Railway in County Durham, it had not impressed the NER who took over in 1900 and spent most of the intervening time in store. On the island it was soon found that its useful-looking 12,800lb tractive effort was at the expense of more weight than the track would accept. Its working career was accordingly brief. With its coal and water capacity reduced it was usable on the Ryde line but was outclassed there by the theoretically less powerful Nos 6 and 8.

Stored by 1914, it was sold in 1917. Its brief career poses questions about whether the company's civil engineer was asked about the purchase in advance, and if so what advice he gave.

The 'Terriers'

The first arrival of this class on the island railways, where they were to be part of the scene for half a century, was the result of the Central's forays into the second-hand market. This time the company struck gold.

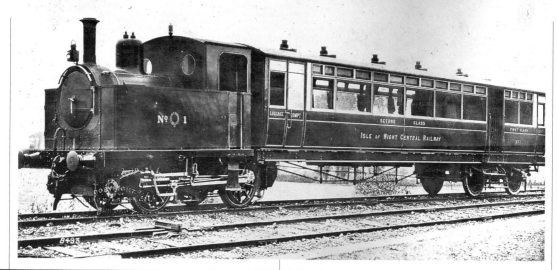

Above:
The IWC's foray into railmotors produced first this neat but rather underpowered assemblage from Hawthorn Leslie in 1906. The loco unit had little power to spare after moving itself and the coach portion. *IAL*

Left:
The railmotor was decommissioned in 1910, the loco portion being given a bunker and being used for works shunting duties. In 1917 it was sold, going through various hands in the northeast. It is seen in 1922, the IWC insignia showing above the current owner's No 8. *LPC*

Below left:
The IWC's second railmotor was home-made, using 0-4-2T No 3 with a bought-in ex-Midland 12-wheel coach. Less successful than No 1, the combination is seen slogging uphill from St Lawrence towards the tunnel. *IAL/Bucknall Coll*

Right:
IWC No 10 was the second 'Terrier' to arrive on the island, in 1900. It is seen shortly before World War 1, still in 'A1' form and with original features including the original short bunker. *IAL/Madgwick Coll*

The 0-6-0T 'Terriers', (originally Class A, later 'A1' and mostly rebuilt as 'A1x' in the early 20th century) first entered traffic in 1872, the first class designed for the Brighton Railway by the illustrious William Stroudley. Eventually 50 strong, the class was intended for smartly-timed London suburban lines, with short journeys punctuated by frequent stops. They were so successful in popularising these lines that they were soon outclassed by increasing train loadings and replaced by larger engines. They promptly found themselves valuable niches on lightly-loaded country branches and as pilot engines at big MPDs, and the class remained fully employed for years.

By the late 1890s the Brighton was finding the class over-large for its needs. A few were scrapped but more found willing purchasers elsewhere, either for industrial use or more commonly on one of the growing number of minor railway companies. Curiously, the neighbouring London & South Western bought a pair, rather than building something new at Eastleigh, when it wanted small locomotives for the Lyme Regis branch. Ironically they proved too big — in the fixed wheelbase that is — and were sold on, one of them finding its way to the Isle of Wight in due course. To conclude the history of the 'Terriers', the class gradually diminished in numbers but lasted into BR days. The last ones were not withdrawn until 1963, with the closure of the Hayling Island branch, and 10 have survived in preservation — not a bad percentage for a class built in the 1870s! Appropriately, two of the survivors have an active life on the Isle of Wight Steam Railway.

In all, eight 'Terriers' were to serve on the Isle of Wight between 1899 and 1949, when the last two returned to the mainland for further service. Four of these were purchased by the IWCR from the Brighton company; each was the subject of anguished negotiations about the price and each was bought through the services of the Southern Counties Rolling Stock Finance Co. All went through Brighton Works before dispatch, where repairs such as new or reconditioned cylinder blocks were fitted as necessary and they were repainted into the current IWCR livery. Despite being delivered in good condition, which must surely have made the purchase prices quite reasonable, they were suffering mechanical problems within a few years, mostly axlebox and crank axle problems, which suggest that the IWCR was determined to recoup its investment while spending a minimum on maintenance; a short-sighted policy best explained by the company's strained finances.

Diminutive to modern eyes the 'Terriers' might be but they were much on a par with the IWCR's 2-4-0Ts and, with smaller wheels and higher boiler pressure, noticeably more powerful, having a tractive effort of around 9,700lb (depending on minor differences between examples). Their only drawback was the limited coal capacity and a

Above left:
IWC No 11 went to the island in 1902, went back to the mainland in 1947, and returned to the island in 1973, where it is now active on the preserved IoW Steam Railway. It is seen here, still with short bunker and coal rails, not long before the 1918 rebuild and reboilering to 'A1x' form. *LPC*

Left:
No 13 *Carisbrooke* was sent to the island in 1927 and received its name in 1929. It is seen in the mid-1930s in 'A1x' form and with extended bunker, very much the classic island 'Terrier'. *LPC*

Above:
Still carrying its Drummond boiler and No 2, but with an extended bunker, ex-FYN *Freshwater* is seen at Ventnor West circa 1930. This 'Terrier', which had one of the most involved careers of its class, has also returned to the island in preservation. *LPC*

simple modification was made to deal with this. Behind the coal bunker was a toolbox. This was removed and the bunker was extended back to the buffer beam, effectively doubling the coal space and making any 'Terrier' that had crossed to the island distinct from its landlubber sisters.

No 9, the first arrival, was ex-LBSC No 75 *Blackwall*. Arriving in 1899, it quickly won the favour of crews and management alike; so much so that three more followed in short order: No 10

(ex No 69 *Peckham*) in 1900, No 11 (ex No 40 *Brighton*) in 1902 and No 12 (ex No 84 *Crowborough*) in 1903.

The 'Terriers' proved ideal for much of the IWCR's requirements, powerful enough to work the train loads for most of the year and yet light enough to operate over the lightly-constructed and engineered lines to Freshwater and Ventnor in particular. When the FYN fell out with the Central in 1913, it not unnaturally was delighted to lay hands on one of the class. This was former LBSC No 46 *Newington*, which had been sold to the LSWR in 1903, becoming No 734. By 1913 it was surplus again and was sold to the FYN, to the companies' mutual satisfaction.

As FYN No 2 it was 'odd man out' in the island fleet, carrying a Drummond boiler with his typical direct-loaded safety valves fore-and-aft on the dome instead of the otherwise standard Salter valves. It also was vacuum braked until after the Grouping, the other island companies opting for air brakes in the wake of the 1889 Regulation of Railways Act. In 1928 as No W2 it was named *Freshwater*, a nice touch, and was renumbered W8 when the 'E1s' arrived and took up the low fleet numbers.

The Southern was just as satisfied with the class for light duties on the island. No 9 was withdrawn, worn out, in 1926 but three more arrived over the next few years: No W3 (renumbered W13) *Carisbrooke* in 1927, No W4 (renumbered W14)

Bembridge in 1929 and No W9 *Fishbourne* in 1930.

Outclassed on goods duties by the 'E1s', four 'Terriers' returned to the mainland in 1936, Nos W9, W10, W12 and W14. No W11 followed in 1947, and the last pair, Nos W8 and W13, in 1949. By then, with the future of the Ventnor West line in doubt, the light goods traffic vanishing and the other lines upgraded to take 'O2s', they had lost their niche. The economics of keeping Ryde Works stocked with spares for a class of two locos was challenged, and they left, to be replaced by the final two 'O2s' to join the island fleet.

Remarkably, four of this fleet have survived among the preserved 'Terriers'. Nos W8 and W11 have returned to the Isle of Wight Steam Railway and Nos W9 and W14 are at the Kent & East Sussex Railway.

FYNR No 1

The last pre-Grouping one-off that deserves mention is the FYN's first purchase, a Manning Wardle 0-6-0ST. Built in 1902 as one of MW's 'Q' class, it was an industrial design that spent its first decade on contractors' construction duties before purchase by the FYN — a sure sign of a railway company in dire straits. That said, it not only gave the island 20 years of service but it was the most modern steam engine seen on the Isle of Wight until the preserved Steam Railway brought over *Invincible* (1915) and *Ajax* (1918) in the 1970s.

Numbered W1 at the Grouping, it was posted in short order to Medina Wharf as resident shunter. Named *Medina* in 1928, it was withdrawn in 1932.

The FYNR owned one other motive power unit, a Drewry petrol railcar. Looking rather like a contemporary charabanc on flanged wheels and even more primitive than the railcars which Col Stephens was to inflict upon his patrons, it could scuttle along at a fair rate. Seating 14, it was used as a standby for steam failures and to provide an 'express' link for Yarmouth ferry passengers to

Newport. It was also available for private hire at one day's notice — an impressive comparison with the three months' notice demanded by today's privatised railway companies! It quite failed to impress the Southern Railway, which withdrew it in 1924, and it was scrapped in 1927 after a brief career as an inspection vehicle.

The Southern's Changes

With the Grouping fast approaching, the nascent Southern Railway's officers had a number of hard, if unofficial, looks at the mixed bag of assets awaiting them on the Isle of Wight. One thing clear was that the motive power situation was parlous to say the least. The IWR's fleet had come through the war in reasonable order (though nothing was less than 40 years old) but the IWCR was not in a good state, even its better machines being more than well worn, while the FYN's two engines were hardly a long-term answer to the line's needs.

Happily the new company would have a ready answer by virtue of its size. With a reserve of spare locomotives, it would not have to contemplate buying or building new for lines which could not afford to pay off such investment; the usual railway accounting principle of writing off the book value of locos and stock over 25 years from new, meant that there was a selection of stock that had years of life left in it but a book value of nil. Good engines and coaches could therefore be sent to improve services on the island lines, without the SR's accountants flinging themselves from the top windows of Waterloo in despair about depreciating assets being tied up in unprofitable locations.

Fortuitously the first big stage of the LSWR's London suburban electrification had recently been completed, making redundant a substantial stock of steam locomotives. Notable among these were two types; the stately '0415s', the Adams 4-4-2 radial tanks, and the chunkier but younger and equally competent Adams 0-4-4T 'O2s'. Both existed in sufficient numbers to meet the needs of the IoW system; both types were considered and, largely on the choice of the Civil Engineer, the 'O2' was chosen. So the stage was set for the remarkable second careers of a class of Victorian tank engines that were to last virtually to the end of BR steam (and at the same time the decision meant the virtual elimination of the '0415s'; the irony is that now just one of each class survives).

Looking at the statistics of the two types as in 1923, the choice is obvious (*see page 46*).

Although smaller, the 'O2' was more powerful. Shorter and lighter, with better acceleration potential, its only disadvantages were the lower water capacity and a rather rougher ride.

Above left:
The FYN's Manning Wardle No 1 carried lined green livery — for some reason a different shade of green to that on No 2! Full lining produced a smart effect. *IAL/Bucknall Coll*

Left:
Under SR ownership No 1 kept its prestigious number and received full SR livery, the word 'Southern' being partly behind the tank handrail. Named *Medina* in 1928, the loco is seen not long before withdrawal in 1932; the cab sidesheets have clearly seen better days! *LPC*

	'0415'	'O2'
Introduced	1882	1889
Length	38ft 8in	30ft 8in
Weight	55 tons 2cwt	46 tons 18cwt
Boiler pressure	160psi	160psi
Cylinders	17½in x 24in	17½in x 24in
Driving wheel diameter	5ft 7in	4ft 10in
Tractive effort	14,920lb	17,235lb
Coal	1 ton	1½ tons
Water	1,200gal	800gal
Wheelbase	29ft 5in	20ft 4in

(Maximum height and width were very similar, as were boiler dimensions, although the 'O2' had a smaller firebox.)

By 1922 the choice had been made and the first pair of 'O2s' were despatched to Eastleigh for conversion to island standards, mainly of course the changing from vacuum to air brake. They arrived at the island, at Ryde Pier Head in fact, in March 1923, still carrying South Western livery; evidence not just of the urgency of getting them out there but of the time it was taking for the details of the new SR livery to be decided. The island's lines could not wait for the deliberations of a committee.

The 'O2s' were an almost immediate success, quickly winning the favour of the crews on the Ryde-Ventnor line, their initial home. They proved to be every bit as good as the largest Beyer

Left:
Apart from the nameplate, No 24 *Calbourne* is in 'as arrived' Isle of Wight condition; Adams boiler, full SR livery, original bunker and Westinghouse brake pump and reservoir fitted at Eastleigh before shipping. *LPC*

Left:
Calbourne in postwar SR condition, carrying lined malachite green with 'sunshine' lettering. The enlarged bunker is evident. *LPC*

Peacock, with that bit extra in hand, largely due to the bigger boiler and extra weight. They were the first of many of their class to grace the island's metals.

The other big change of that first grouped year was the renumbering of the island's stock into a single series. The FYN duo had the lowest slot, followed by the Central's locos and then the IWR's fleet, given numbers for the first time in their lives. The 'O2s' were numbered above them, commencing with the first two arrivals, 19 and 20. Numbers began at No 1 (or W1; the 'W' prefix appeared and vanished at times over the years) and established the tradition of the island having fleet numbers distinct from the SR, and later BR, main list. The old tradition still applied that as locos were scrapped, their numbers were reissued (a habit which the SR was later to abandon on the mainland); thus the 'E1s' took Nos 1-4 and later 'Terrier' arrivals filled up the withdrawn IWCR numbers.

'O2' arrivals continued at a rate of two or three in most years into the mid-1930s, although the last two actually arrived in 1949 as replacements for the last two 'Terriers'.

The four 'E1s' were the next Southern import to the island. Another ex-Brighton class of Stroudley design, they were in many ways 'big sisters' of the 'Terriers', though in size and power terms they were only a little below the LMS's ubiquitous '3F' 0-6-0Ts. For comparison, they weighed 44 tons 3cwt and had a tractive effort of 18,560lb, against the 'Jinties' 49 tons 10cwt and 20,835lb.

Based at Newport, they were sent to the island mainly as goods engines and a lot of their time was spent in shunting at, and transporting coal

from, Medina Wharf. However they were perfectly good passenger engines too and could take over from an 'O2' without batting an eyelid. They were commonly used to haul the 'Tourist', Ventnor to Freshwater in the mornings and back in the evenings, summer weekdays.

The collapse of goods traffic in the early 1950s was their death-knell and they were withdrawn from 1956 onwards, when it was decided that the 'O2s' could cope with what freight traffic remained.

One other item of motive power deserves mention. This is *Midget*, the Ryde Works man-powered shunter. *Midget* was designed by MacLeod to expedite light shunting at the works. Basically a flat trolley, its wheels were given coupling rods and on the deck was a contraption of two large wheels with handles, a bit like outsize mangle wheels or something from a chocolate-box picture of a well. Two men wound away at these wheels and through chains and gears *Midget* edged forward, dragging a coach, or perhaps an engine, behind it. Not surprisingly, its career did not long outlast the promotion of its creator to Waterloo!

The 'O2s'

In all, 23 'O2s' served on the island. Nos W19-W32 arrived in almost annual batches from 1923-28, Nos W17 and W18 in 1930, Nos W14-16 and W33 in 1936 and W34-6 after the war. The four poorest examples were withdrawn in 1955/6, in the wake of line closures, and withdrawals continued in a steady trickle, although 14 lasted into 1966.

Apart from the numbering, and from 1928 the names, there were several distinctive differences

from their mainland sisters. All carried Westinghouse air brake pumps on the left side of the smokebox and air reservoirs on the left tank top, there being no room for the conventional location around or within the frames. Most striking was the enlarged coal bunker, first fitted in 1932 and soon applied to the whole fleet. The 'Macleod Improved Bunker' as that Island Assistant was proud to call it, reached higher up the cab back and was flared out over the rear bufferbeam as far as practicable. It increased coal capacity from 1½ tons to 3¼ tons, which achieved the purpose of

allowing a loco to work one of the full, 200-mile summer Saturday shifts without having to head back to St Johns Road for more coal.

St Johns Road Works and shed took loving care of their charges, which were always maintained to the best possible standard and turned out smartly. Only in the last few years were there signs of disillusion, and then the declining condition of the fleet owed more to the wearing out of irreplaceable parts than lack of effort by Works staff. Cracked frames, wonky back bogies and leaking Westinghouse pumps were dealt with as

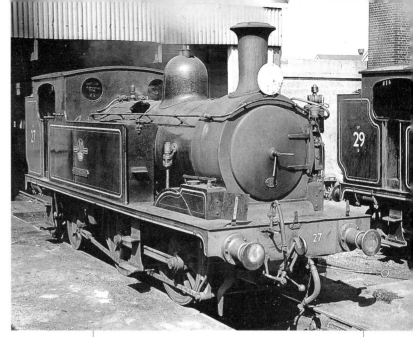

well as possible, with the worst affected locos nursed along and only sent out at peak service times.

The first arrivals were fitted with Drummond boilers rather than the original Adams type, but as soon as 'O2s' with Adams boilers arrived the crews insisted that they were better, the Drummond type being shy steamers. Replacement Adams boilers were duly fitted, though Drummond ones turned up from time to time, depending what Eastleigh had available when an engine was being overhauled for shipping to the island, or what was in stock when an island boiler needed replacement. A Drummond boiler was a sure sign that an engine could expect an easier life than its colleagues, for the crews would shun it whenever possible.

By the time of their withdrawal, many of the class had run around 1½ million miles in mainland and island service. In some 70 years they must have repaid their original cost many times over.

The 'E1s'

Stroudley's standard short-haul goods engine had one disadvantage for passenger work. Their wheels were balanced to give least stress to the running gear at low speeds, but when put on passenger duty this produced an unpleasant fore-and-aft feeling in the train as speed increased. In the 1880s they were known as the 'Seasick Tanks' by offended passengers.

Notwithstanding, the island's quartet were turned out in SR passenger livery by Eastleigh before despatch, Nos W1-W3 (*Medina, Yarmouth* and *Ryde*) in 1932 and No W4 *Wroxall* a year later. *Ryde* Works adjusted *Wroxall's* wheel

balance that autumn and the others had similar treatment as they next went through works.

Spending their time mostly on goods work, the 'E1s' had a relatively low profile among enthusiasts, though their appearance as standby passenger power and regular working of the heavily-loaded 'Tourist' were duly appreciated. Following Nationalisation they were painted in the drab unlined black goods livery. By then the coal traffic was starting to fall away and other goods trade was fast vanishing. Following a decision that the 'O2s' could cope with what remained, the 'E1s' were withdrawn, No W2 going first in 1956, and the last survivor W4 in 1960. Briefly considered by members of the infant Bluebell Railway, it was described as 'a rusted wreck', which was, sadly, enough to put off nascent preservationists.

Might-have-beens

Two episodes deserve mention to conclude this review.

Immediately after World War 2 it was apparent to the SR that the 'O2s' needed help; not yet because they were worn out but because the peak traffic demands were exceeding their powers. Consideration was given to sending some larger locomotives to take the lion's share of the strain. Bearing in mind the system's physical constraints, the ex-LBSC Billinton 0-6-2T 'E4s' seemed most suitable.

Some nine tons heavier than an 'O2' on the same number of axles, with similar sized wheels, cylinders and theoretical power, the 'E4' seems such a strange choice that it shows how limited the possibilities were! Its one real

'02' line-ups — three MPD scenes

Above:
Nos 22 *Brading*, 32 *Bonchurch*, 24 *Calbourne* and 17 *Seaview* in Ryde MPD yard in the early 1930s. *IAL*

Left:
No time was wasted on the island in changing the fleet from wartime black to full Bulleid livery but Nos 23 *Totland*, 15 *Cowes* and 16 *Ventnor*, seen inside Ryde shed on 17 July 1947, are still in unlined black with green-shaded lettering. *A. F. Cook*

Below:
Nos 28 *Ashey*, 24 *Calbourne* and 25 *Godshill* make a smart looking trio at Ryde in December 1960. *M. Pope*

advantage was the extra adhesive power given by the third coupled axle and the extra weight. The fact that it could be considered also shows how much the island system had been improved since 1923.

No 2510 was selected, modified for island service and arrived in early 1947. It proved unpopular from the start, being accused of damaging the track and being heavy on fuel and water while doing little that an 'O2' could not. It soon found itself reduced in status to spare engine at Newport, about as low as one could get on the island roster, and was returned to the mainland after little more than two years.

To what extent it was really unsuitable and how much was owed to the conservatism of island footplate crews must be a matter for conjecture. Both views have been expressed by former island railwaymen. Certainly on paper it showed little improvement over the 'O2s'; on the other hand a sole example of a class is rarely popular in an otherwise homogeneous fleet.[2]

Ten years later the problem arose again. Although the traffic was not what it had been, a summer Saturday could still see the familiar heavy crowds on the Ryde-Ventnor line and some of the 'O2s' were by now showing signs of distress. Modernising with BR Standard Class 2 tanks was proposed and in March 1960 2-6-2T

[2] Again, the same situation exists on the Isle of Man, where the solitary Dübs 0-6-0T Caledonia, far from being a rose among the Beyer Peacock 2-4-0T thorns, has always been unpopular, with firemen more than with drivers. This is still true today.

No 84020 went to Eastleigh for modifications, mainly trimming the height by a few inches. The project was stopped before it had got very far, when BR decided on a far more radical solution to the island system's problems — elimination. Until closure of as much as possible could be arranged, the 'O2s' were left to continue unassisted.

There is a sweet irony in that it is now the preservationists who are taking the wheel full circle. In 1997 the IoW Steam Railway agreed with the owners of the two Ivatt 2-6-2Ts under restoration at Quainton Road, Nos 41298 and 41313, to transfer them to the island to operate on the preserved line, relieving the load on the elderly *Calbourne* in a more appropriate way than a Hunslet 'Austerity'. The Ivatt class was a broadly identical predecessor of the BR Class 2 tank design. Whether the newcomers will be numbered W37 and W38 remains to be seen.

Liveries

Inevitably locomotive liveries changed over the years. The most variety was to be seen on the Central, which as the C&N commenced operations with a lined light blue colour scheme. Later this was changed to 'metallic red', which apparently was a rich colour rather than the bright, shiny red described as 'metallic' by modern car painters. A badge in garter form carried the company's name and loco number. This changed to the company name in full and later just the initials.

Later the Central adopted a black livery, lined rather than too plain, which lasted until the Grouping. The IWR by contrast adopted a red

Right:
'E1' No 4 *Wroxall* shows its SR passenger green livery to advantage at Newport in the mid-1930s. The original intention had been to paint the island foursome in SR goods black, as was the case for most of their mainland sisters. *LPC*

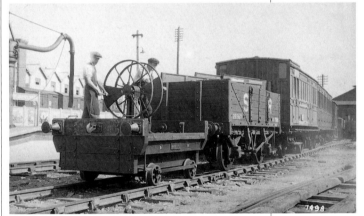

Above:
Plain black was soon to claim the
'E1s' however, and remained the
case under BR ownership, as seen
here on No 1 *Medina*, shunting at
Sandown in the early 1950s.
Brian Morrison

Left:
MacLeod's Ryde Works shunter,
Midget, in action. *IAL*

livery not far removed from Midland Red, and
stuck with it until Grouping.

With only two locomotives to call its own, the
FYN managed to avoid any standardisation at all,
painting them in two different shades of green.
Perhaps it would be wrong to imply criticism in
this; after all, an increasing number of preserved
railways are now avoiding a standard livery, on the
grounds that young passengers who have had a
ride behind one engine want to come back for a
trip behind one of the others. Perhaps the FYN
simply recognised a good marketing ploy years
before other railways?

With the arrival of the SR, all this changed for
the uniformity of green. Maunsell's dark green,
with its usual changes, came first. The Bulleid era,
with its malachite green and sunshine lettering,
did not reach the island before the outbreak of
war. A change to plain black was the inevitable
result of World War 2, with Bulleid lettering
shaded green. However, malachite green began
to creep in by early 1945 and by that summer,
when the island began to experience its first

tourist season for six years, there was a fleet of
bright green locomotives waiting to meet arrivals
at Ryde Pier Head. The later reversion to black
under BR was inevitable — by no stretch of the
imagination could the island be described as
running express locomotives — but at least it was
lined and at least the MPD staff's pride in the fleet
kept them looking immaculate until the last
season or so. Only the 'E1s' carried the sombre
unlined black livery, a move which took them
even further away from the public eye in their last
years.

Right:
Finale for the 'O2s'. The sorry sight of nine of the
veterans lined up at Newport awaiting scrapping.
Heading the queue is No 27 *Merstone,* which had
dragged the others from the main platform roads into
the Freshwater yard on 18 April 1967, then Nos 20, 16,
35, 28, 17, 33, 14 and 22 nearest the camera. What
price for such a matching set of Victorian engines
these days? *IAL*

The Island 'O2s'

IoW No	Name	LSWR/SR No	Built	Trans to IoW	Withdrawn
W14	Fishbourne	178	1889	5/1936	1966
W15	Cowes	195	1890	5/1936	1956
W16	Ventnor	217	1892	5/1936	1966
W17	Seaview	208	1891	5/1930	1966
W18	Ningwood	220	1892	5/1930	1965
W19	Osborne	206	1891	5/1923	1955
W20	Shanklin	211	1892	5/1923	1966
W21	Sandown	205	1891	6/1924	1966
W22	Brading	215	1892	6/1924	1966
W23	Totland	188	1890	4/1925	1955
W24	Calbourne	209	1891	4/1925	*1967
W25	Godshill	190	1890	6/1925	1962
W26	Whitwell	210	1891	6/1925	1966
W27	Merstone	184	1890	3/1926	1966
W28	Ashey	186	1890	3/1926	1966
W29	Alverstone	202	1891	4/1926	1966
W30	Shorwell	219	1892	4/1926	1965
W31	Chale	180	1890	5/1927	1967
W32	Bonchurch	226	1892	5/1928	1964
W33	Bembridge	218	1892	5/1936	1966
W34	Newport	201	1891	4/1947	1955
W35	Freshwater	181	1890	4/1949	1966
W36	Carisbrooke	198	1891	4/1949	1964

* — Acquired for preservation.

In all, 23 of the total class of 60 'O2s' worked on the Isle of Wight

Island 'Terriers'

LBSC No & Name	Built	Trans IoW	IoW owner /No/Name	SR No/ ReNo/name	Ret mainland	Withdrawn
75 Blackwall	1872	1899	IWC/9/Carisbrooke	W9	—	1926
69 Peckham	1874	1900	IWC/10/Cowes	W10/—/Cowes	1936	1936
40 Brighton	1878	1902	IWC/11/Newport	W11/—/Newport	1947	*1963
84 Crowborough	1880	1903	IWC/12/Ventnor	W12/—/Ventnor	1936	1936
46 Newington	1876	1913	FYN/2/Freshwater	W2/W8/Freshwater	1949	*1963
77 Wonersh	1880	1927	—	W3/W13 Carisbrooke	1949	1959
78 Knowle	1880	1929	—	W4/W14/Bembridge	1936	**1963
50 Whitechapel	1876	1930	—	W9/—/Fishbourne	1936	**1963

* — Preserved, Isle of Wight Steam Railway
** — Preserved, Kent & East Sussex Railway

Island 'E1s'

LBSC No & Name	Built	Trans to IoW	IoW No & Name	Withdrawn
136 Brindisi	1879	1932	W1 Medina	1957
152 Hungary	1880	1932	W2 Yarmouth	1956
154 Madrid	1881	1932	W3 Ryde	1959
131 Gournay	1878	1933	W4 Wroxall	1960

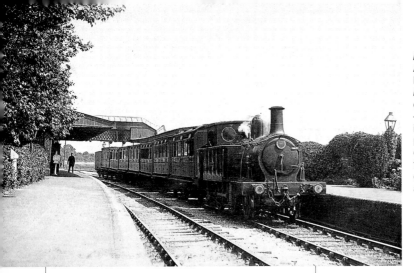

Left:
An early 20th-century view of an IWR train at Brading behind *Bonchurch*. Although all the stock comes from one builder — Oldbury — the train is anything but uniform in appearance. The wavy long-profile of the train deserves comment too; whether due to poor track or tired springs, it is not calculated to inspire confidence among passengers. *LPC*

Left:
Bonchurch heads briskly uphill near Wroxall with a train of assorted IWR coaches. Just two pairs of vehicles match and even they are not marshalled together.
IAL/Bucknall Coll

Below:
IWC No 4 heads a typical mix of four-wheelers on a Ryde-Newport train in the last years of the company's existence.
IAL/Bucknall Coll

Rolling Stock

Like motive power, the rolling stock history of the Isle of Wight railways falls into several distinct eras, with not too much blurring at the edges. Each time that it was decided that improvements must be made, things would happen with commendable promptness, and the new arrivals would give years of satisfactory service before the inevitable slither into genteel decline.

The first era was by far the longest, the 60 years from the first opening to the Grouping. These years were typified by the companies' tight budgets, which conspired with rising passenger figures and the dilapidation of existing stock to force them into the second-hand market. Only the IWR was able to buy new from the builders on a regular basis, and apart from its first purchases the IWCR managed this only twice, the second time ending up with a bit of a white elephant, a steam railmotor set.

The Pre-Grouping Years

The Isle of Wight Railway had a long association with the Oldbury Railway Carriage Co, which supplied several batches of four-wheelers. Later it persuaded the IWR to buy three vehicles from the Golden Valley Railway, which had ended up back on its hands after that line had folded. The two coaches and a van spent much of their time on the Bembridge branch, the coaches being instantly recognisable for their end balconies and six-wheel chassis, with the middle axleboxes suspended from the outside of the frames to give extra sideplay.

For later purchases the IWR turned to the second-hand market and bought a number of coaches from the North London Railway. These were followed just before World War 1 by 18 vehicles from the Metropolitan Railway. These were eight-wheelers and the gullible could be deluded into thinking they were bogie coaches. In fact the running gear was attached direct to the mainframes, giving a rigid wheelbase, although plenty of controlled sideplay was allowed. They dated from the days when bogie coaches were just becoming popular and alternative ways of supporting longer coach bodies were being investigated by companies with faith in their track quality.

The type must have been quite successful for they managed a respectable career on the Metropolitan. The IWR's purchases quickly became the line's favoured stock. They were not withdrawn until the 1930s and even then some entered a third incarnation — holiday cottages. Some survive in this role even now.

The IWR adopted a 'varnished hardwood' finish for its stock; quite common in the 1860s, it was becoming more unusual in the 1920s, when it finally succumbed to brushloads of SR green.

After the earliest purchases by the Cowes & Newport and the IW(NJ)R, the Isle of Wight Central and its constituents relied almost totally on the second-hand market. This was not necessarily so bad for passengers as it might sound, for in an era where standards of passenger comfort were advancing fast, some real bargains were to be found by a railway shopping for redundant stock if it could move quickly enough. Unfortunately the Central did not always have the money available at the right time.

A mixed bag gradually evolved through the 1880s and early 1890s, including for instance several vehicles bought from the North London Railway and a short rake of ex-LBSC four-wheelers. In 1890 the company surprised many people, including probably itself, by buying two new bogie coaches from Lancaster Carriage & Wagon, but then the reaction set in and there was a long gap before the next purchases of note, the first of a series of second-hand coaches from the LSWR. The Central bought 28 of these around the turn of the century, mainly replacing some of the real relics that passengers were objecting to travelling in.

The railmotor and the ex-Midland Railway coach bought to provide a home-made 'lash-up' second set, added two more bogie coaches to stock in the Edwardian era, soon being available for normal use as the railmotor concept proved itself as flawed on the island as elsewhere. The final purchase of note before the Grouping was when the Central was reduced to buying some Oldbury withdrawals from the IWR in the war years.

The net result of all this was that an IWCR train presented a varied appearance as it passed by. Roof line and profile, panelling, length and width — none were standard. The livery was little better; it was officially varnished teak but in practice not all the coaches had teak skins, so there was some variation in the hue of varnished hardwood. It appears that some of the second-hand stock arrived painted and was repainted brown to vaguely match the rest, being stripped back for a varnished wood finish at its first overhaul at Newport. The railmotor stock was red with cream

Top:
Some evidence of standardisation in this view of an IWC Cowes train at Newport circa 1910. The first four coaches behind the 'Terrier' are near-matching LSWR stock. *LPC*

Above:
First fruits of the SR regime; order and improved stock. Four four-wheel ex-LBSC Billinton coaches at Newport, with a set number on the end, indicating that the coaches were expected to be kept together for some considerable time. A pair of ex-LCDR four-wheelers stand beyond the set. *IAL/Madgwick Coll*

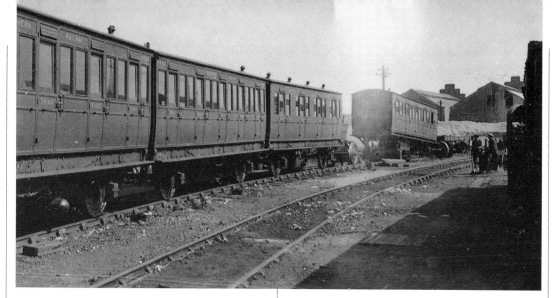

Above:
A set of ex-LCDR six-wheel stock, converted to four-wheelers for island service, at Newport in the late 1920s. Apparently the brake end vehicle is undergoing axlebox attention. *A. B. MacLeod/IAL*

trimmings and later presented a jarring note when mixed with other coaches.

The FYN in 1913 was less concerned with precisely what coaches it got than with the urgency of getting anything at all. Seven four-wheelers were duly purchased from the Great Central, all some 30 years old. It also bought five coaches from the IWCR, not so much because it wanted to but because it had to, under the terms of the rescinded working agreement! The Central took the view, not unnaturally, that as it had had to purchase extra stock for working FYN services, it should be entitled to sell them to any future operator.

FYN stock was also finished in a varnished teak livery. In one respect however, it differed from the other lines on the island; in accord with its tradition of being different (almost for the sake of it, it sometimes seems) it adopted the vacuum brake, while its neighbours had standardised on air brakes — though it was only after considerable procrastination that the entire IWCR fleet was fitted to conform with the 1889 Act.

The Southern and Afterwards

Although the Southern Railway made an almost immediate decision that something had to be done, and quickly, about the Isle of Wight stock, finding a solution was not so easy. SR coaching policy had two major strands; suburban electrification and modernising the main line expresses. Hardly any stock was built new for minor lines and any ageing bodies with some life left in them were likely to find themselves reused on new chassis (electric unit ones as often as not) rather than being declared redundant.

However, some not-too-geriatric stock was released for the island, deliveries beginning in time for the 1923 season. First came nine early bogie coaches from the LSWR; around 40 years old on arrival, they must still have been a revelation to islanders — electric light guaranteed, whichever coach you got into, and steam heating for the first time! This last might have been a severe shock to the boilers of elderly locomotives but to island residents it was a sign that the SR was really taking an interest in them and their railway. This stock was used to revolutionise the former IWCR main lines.

These were followed by several batches of ex-LBSC and then ex-LCDR stock, all four-wheelers (the six-wheel LCDR coaches had had their central axles removed), which arrived through the 1920s and came to dominate the system, including the prestigious Ventnor line. As each batch arrived, further relics were withdrawn.

The new stock was certainly an improvement on what it replaced (most of which looked like it had been in service since Adam was a lad) but it was not really in keeping with the general image that the SR was trying to project. Travellers to this keenly promoted 'premier holiday isle' crossed the Solent to find a train waiting which was undeniably from a previous era. Non-bogie stock was a real rarity on the mainland by then, the sort of thing you would only meet on bank holiday excursions. The shiny SR green paint only emphasised the anachronism.

Within seven years something more was done; beginning in 1930 there was an influx of ex-London, Chatham & Dover bogie stock. Displaced

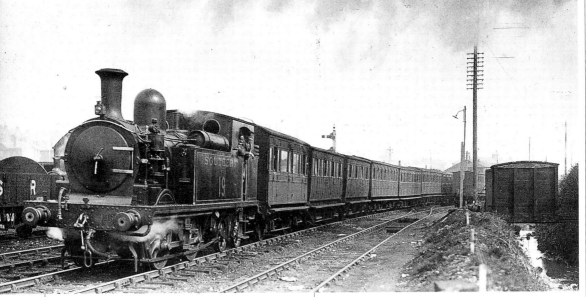

from Kent lines by 'cascading' of stock caused by the arrival of the new Maunsell main line stock, it would normally have been scrapped but MacLeod grabbed it. Though old and well-used, it at least looked to the casual eye much like any minor SR route could offer. At last the island's 'main lines' could offer trains that looked reasonably up to date. In all, 40 assorted ex-LCDR coaches were transferred to the island, making a considerable difference to passenger facilities.

Further electrification on the mainland allowed an influx of ex-LBSCR coaches from 1934 onwards and the non-bogie stock could be virtually eliminated. The old LSWR bogie coaches, by now about 50 years old, were also withdrawn at this time. Doubtless more would have followed but the outbreak of war put everything on hold.

This Brighton stock was in some cases quite recent; built in the 1900s and later, some batches were actually completed post-Grouping and when sent to the island were less than 15 years old. By the time the last arrived in 1939, there were 62 of them on Isle of Wight metals; despite coincident withdrawals, the number of available seats had

Above left:
Shortly after the Grouping, 'O2' No 22 is seen on the Ventnor line with a classic late-period IWR train. The fourth, fifth and sixth coaches are ex-Metropolitan eight-wheel stock. *LPC*

Left:
No 19, one of the first pair of 'O2s' to arrive on the island, leaves St Johns Road with a train of four- and eight-wheel IWR stock. *W. H. Whitworth*

Above:
In 1938 and 1947 several ex-LBSC push-pull bogie coaches were transferred to the island. One of them, probably No 6987, is seen leaving Ventnor West, propelled by No 8, in April 1949. *J. H. Aston*

risen considerably through the 1930s, indicative of the build-up of summer holiday traffic.

From 1945 things quickly returned to normal and it became clear that the ex-LCDR stock could not last much longer. Much of it had been stored during the war, which had done nothing to slow the deterioration.

Now a new difficulty arose in finding suitable replacements; there were not that many coaches around that were small enough to fit! The island lines had a restricted loading gauge, a legacy of being built on the cheap. This had not been

unusual for mid-Victorian minor lines but while most of those on the mainland had been brought up to standard in the intervening years, the island lines had been left alone. In height terms the loading gauge was nearly a foot lower than the mainland standard and sharp curves allied with the closeness of lineside structures (bridges, platforms and so on) placed a limit on the length of coaches that could be used. Send over a modern, long coach and its mid-section would be too close to these structures on the inside of curves. Apart from that, the Southampton floating crane was still the only economic way of bringing new stock to the island and that too had length restrictions.

So recourse had to be had to some of the oldest remaining stock, in the shape of Edwardian SECR coaches. Most of these came from the famous 'birdcage' sets, which got their name from the raised section of roof over the guard's vans, giving a lookout view along the top of the train. Even so, to fit the island loading gauge, these birdcage lookouts had to go and even the torpedo ventilators on the roofs had to be removed. The drastic treatment did not stop there, for this stock was modern enough to include lavatory compartments. Toilets on the island's short journeys were seen as an unnecessary luxury, so they were converted into extra seating. This gave some

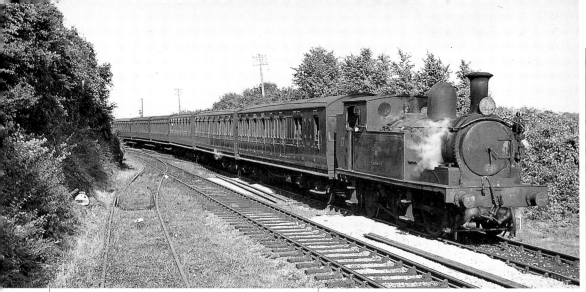

Above:
Set 497, a mixture of LBSC and SECR stock, berthed in the siding south of Brading station on 3 September 1966. Even this late in the steam era, the paintwork is clean enough to throw a good reflection. *A. D. McIntyre*

Left:
One of the ex-SECR lavatory composites, which had their central compartments and lavatories converted into a small saloon. Some of the body panelling has been plated over, where decay was starting to gain the upper hand. *IAL*

Left:
A BR train of six bogie coaches, the maximum permitted, leaving Brading for Shanklin on 3 September 1966. To stay within the 'O2s' load limit, a six-coach train had to include at least two LBSC coaches, which were lighter than the SECR stock. The first three of No 27 *Merstone's* train are ex-LBSC, identifiable by their arc roofs. *J. Scrace*

Right:
SECR third No 2442 was the last steam-stock coach to pass through Ryde Works. Seen here in the C&W shop with its side panelling almost totally replaced by sheet metal, the vehicle looks quite up to date for the mid-1960s. *Dr J. Mackett*

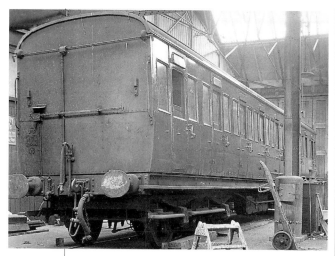

coaches a rather claustrophobic coupé compartment (seats on one side only), and some composites, which had central lavatories flanked by first class compartments, gained small saloon sections instead, two compartments and the separating lavatories being knocked into one, with seats round the edge. Other coaches received equally drastic treatment, with compartments being removed to increase luggage space. These alterations resulted in the coaches being barely recognisable from their previous forms but — to the cognoscenti — unmistakably Isle of Wight stock.

With 40 LCDR coaches to replace and more space being given in the SECR arrivals for luggage, a sizeable fleet was needed to retain the system's seating capacity and 52 of these coaches were sent over, after the most drastic surgery ever given to coaches destined for the island. They, with the Brighton stock, were to last to the end of the old order in 1966, although their numbers gradually declined as closures rendered stock redundant. However, a good mix of both types remained until the end of 1966, partly because a full six-coach load was only below the weight limit if it included three Brighton coaches and partly because the blend of accommodation and luggage space was on quite a fine calculation.

Tight budgets brought about another phenomenon at this time, plated sides. The plating over of sections of a panelled coach body that had deteriorated beyond recall had been island practice for some years but from the late 1940s to the 1960s it became elevated to a local art form. In some cases, where a coach was completely, or almost, de-panelled and given a flush metal exterior, it could look quite smart and up-to-date, particularly when smartly painted. Too often though, it was piecemeal and looked exactly what it was — a bodge to keep a crumbling coach in traffic.

With the end in sight for steam operation, the coaching situation was getting quite frantic. Closures had eased the problem by allowing the worst stock to be scrapped and not replaced but a long-term solution was needed. On the mainland there was now nothing left that could be adapted to fit the island loading gauge.

It was this dilemma that forced the idea of using London Underground stock to be considered. There, and only there, could coaches small enough to fit the existing IoW loading gauge be found. However the Underground, like the Southern in the past, was not flush with spare stock for sale. The best it was prepared to offer was superannuated tube trains being replaced by new deliveries.

And so the electrified Isle of Wight line was equipped with rolling stock nearly as old as some of the steam stock it replaced. Happily a fair sample of the earlier stock was saved for preservation and, as older specimens are rescued and restored, a broad cross-section of the steam age coaching stock of the island is presented. It seems rather sad though that a three-car electric set was not also kept when finally withdrawn in 1989, as a reminder of a 23-year era of island transport.

The livery history of the system from 1923 to 1966 was predominantly green. First came the rich Southern green of the Maunsell era, with its elaborate lining out and lettering, that became somewhat simplified over the years. With the arrival of Bulleid this changed to the brighter, almost harsh, malachite green and 'sunshine' style lettering, although the war dramatically slowed down the repainting programme.

By the time everything was in the new green and lettering, it was almost time to change again with the arrival of British Railways; new numbering and new lettering but the green lasted for a while.

Above:
No 20 *Shanklin* runs into Haven Street with the daily Ryde-Ventnor goods on 8 April 1961. By then the island's freight traffic was almost entirely coal — a good part of it for railway consumption. *J. C. Haydon*

Left:
One of the ex-LSWR 10-ton road vans (combined guards and goods vans) sent to the island in the 1920s. The type became almost universal on island goods trains. *IAL*

Corporate liveries were agreed by 1950 and the Isle of Wight stock duly began to appear in the bright red (crimson) non-corridor livery. If a dramatic change, at least it was smart and, as ever on the Isle of Wight Railways, it was well applied. The island's relatively small fleet was soon fully repainted and presented a more uniform image to passengers than many mainland trains did; but another change was soon on the way, the reversion to green in 1956, when the Southern Region was allowed to adopt its own livery, the excuse being that it allowed uniformity with the large electric fleet which was already green. This hardly applied on the island but the chance was not missed and soon the new green, not very different from malachite, was the dominant stock colour. It lasted until the end, the arrival of rail blue coinciding with the introduction of electric services in 1967.

Goods Stock

Like any Victorian system, the Isle of Wight lines were originally well provided with goods stock and sidings to keep it on. Literally hundreds of wagons and vans graced the network. In variety they were limited however, for the sufficient reason that the traffic available was restricted. Agricultural produce and stock, assorted bulky but small-scale deliveries and the one big item — transport of coal — dominated the scene. The specialist wagon types that evolved on the mainland system were hardly needed here. When special circumstances did arise, the railways expected their workshops to come up with a conversion to suit.

Like the passenger stock, the early wagons gave years of faithful service and by the Grouping were far past their prime. Again, replacement stock was shipped in and over the years the island became a sort of railway Valhalla for elderly goods stock. Wooden-bodied open trucks of various shapes, sizes and origins were in daily use there long after steel-bodied replacements had swept them aside on the main system. The same applied to vans and brake vans. A typical 1950s goods train on the Isle of Wight resembled a West Country pick-up goods in the latter days of the LSWR.

One crucial reason for this was of course the virtual collapse of the goods business after World War 2, when a fast growth in lorry numbers saw off the railway service with its expensive multiple transhipments and other problems. Only the coal traffic survived and that was slowly whittled away during the 1950s.

In its late SR heyday, however, the system could boast over 500 open wagons — practically 10 per route mile. Not that this was really a subject for boasting; rather it showed the great weakness of railway freight operations. The wagons spent most of their time standing idle, awaiting loading or unloading and obstructing sidings, rather than getting on with their supposed job of actually moving cargoes from place to place. No wonder the unit costs were high and no wonder the more cut-throat attitudes of road hauliers made them such deadly competitors. While a coal merchant would expect, indeed insist, that the railway give him a few days to unload a wagon, he would never be brave enough to suggest the same to the driver of a lorry. And as road traffic modernised when the railways could not afford to, the self-tipping lorry soon made even the briefest of unloading delays unnecessary, while railway wagons still had to be laboriously shovelled out by hand. By the early 1960s the main freight traffic on the railway was coal from

Medina Wharf to Ryde MPD and the wagon fleet had been whittled down accordingly.

Few remained at the end and they were in a poor condition. Happily a small representative selection was saved by the preservationists. As the hard-pressed Carriage & Wagon Department at Haven Street finds spare time from bringing the revenue-earning passenger stock up to standard, goods stock projects are tackled and slowly an IoW goods train is taking shape again.

Below:
The pre-Grouping goods fleet was largely worn out by the early 1920s and was almost totally replaced by SR stock. This ex-IWR 12-ton wagon was one of the few survivors, seeing out its last years transferred to departmental service. *IAL*

Bottom:
No 31 *Chale* heads away from Medina Wharf for Newport with the afternoon freight train on 8 June 1961. *K. L. Cook*

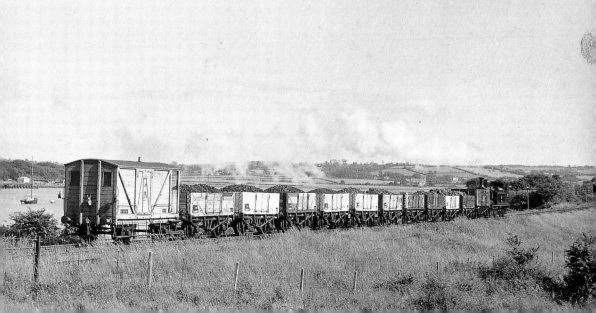

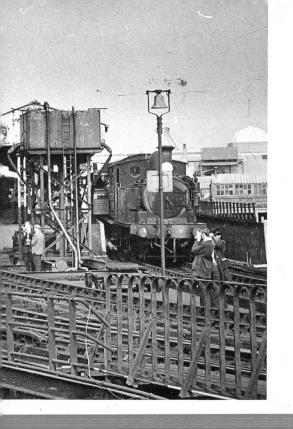

4

The Routes

Most passengers on the Isle of Wight system started — or ended — their journeys at Ryde Pier Head. Of these, the bulk travelled on the Ventnor line, so let us commence our brief tour of the system with this line, especially as it is the route where part of the story can be written in the present tense.

The pierhead itself is a shadow of its former self, with the big, dome-roofed ballroom now but a memory and the space where thousands of waiting passengers once milled turned over to car parking for a privileged minority. The fast and frequent catamaran service has replaced forever the days when up to four steamers at once would be tied up to the landing stages but somehow they lack quite the *style* that the old boats had.

Pier Head station once had four platforms that witnessed hectic activity on a regular basis, with up to six arrivals and six departures per hour on summer Saturdays. A signalbox and a scissors crossover gave maximum flexibility, most necessary for managing a passenger train movement every 5min or so, plus the transfer of released locomotives from behind the last train to leave to the front of the next one; there was no time for shunting stock, and with six-coach trains, not really much room either. Now the station is reduced to two platforms, each on a single line isolated from the other until Esplanade station is passed. The old down line is evidently seldom if ever used and indeed the points layout at Esplanade makes it suitable for special, emergency, or shuttle-service use only.

The electric multiple-units hum in and out with less fuss and more efficiency than their forebears

but also without the sense of occasion that made arrival at Ryde for the start of a holiday so memorable. Station buildings and staff are largely memories, too. It is now assumed that passengers arrive booked through to Esplanade at least, and where once caged trucks of luggage were unloaded from steamers and wheeled into capacious luggage vans, you are now expected, like everywhere else, to struggle along with your own baggage. Ah, the march of progress!

A quick run down the near-half-mile of the pier line and a sharp left-hander into Esplanade station, still largely recognisable as its former self. Though once all was rigidly up and down lines, now only the up platform is in normal use. A toot on the whistle (a mellow hooter in steam days, a pleasing chime whistle on the electrics — a nice touch of independence from main line air-horn practice!) and the train sets off, plunging down a steep grade into Esplanade Tunnel.

The tunnel is technically a covered way, built by cut-and-cover rather than bored, and is quite shallow. Despite this it is below high tide level and the pumping station remains in use beside Esplanade station. It sees less use than before, as advantage was taken of the reduced height of the electric stock to raise the tunnel floor in 1967. Sadly, this will preclude the return of *Calbourne* to Pier Head, even if, as expected, the preserved line is physically joined to the electric route in the future. A 'Terrier' might fit though...

Out of the 391yd tunnel and a sweeping curve turns the line southwards towards St Johns Road station, 1¼ miles from Pier Head. The three platforms are now two; the old down loop platform is now a carriage siding, in regular use for the cleaning of stock. The main wooden building survives as do the canopies, though shortened, still bearing in their stanchion spandrels the 'IWR' monogram. St Johns Road is now the administrative, engineering and signalling centre for the line as well as the stock depot. It has always been the locomotive HQ and the remains of early works buildings can be seen alongside the modernised repair shed. Opposite, the former steam MPD has disappeared without trace. The signalbox remains, controlling the whole line now.

Above left:
Ryde Pier Head, the focus of many journeys on the island's railways, could be a busy place. On 3 October 1965 No 24 *Calbourne* leaves with the LCGB 'Vectis Farewell' railtour, while two other 'O2s' wait with Cowes and Ventnor trains. *John H. Bird*

Left:
A Ventnor train heads away from Pier Head on 28 August 1964. *M. Dunnett*

Track plan of Ryde Tunnel-Pier Head. All track plans are as at 1947-48.

To St John's Road

Track plan of Ryde St Johns Road and Smallbrook.

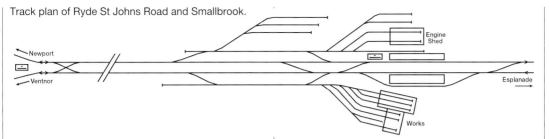

Left:
Esplanade station about the turn of the century, with an IWC train for Pier Head passing the impressive bracket signal. *IAL/Bucknall Coll*

Bottom left:
'O2' No 33 *Bembridge* heads a Ventnor train out of Esplanade station and down the steep grade into the tunnel in August 1959. *P. J. Lynch*

Below:
St Johns Road looking south in pre-Grouping days, when the tracks were signalled for the independent parallel single lines to Smallbrook. *LPC*

It began life at Waterloo before moving to the island in the 1920s, another example of the island system's status as 'Second-hand Rose'.

From here in the old days, trains would diverge onto one of the two parallel single lines to Smallbrook, nearly a mile away, Ventnor trains taking the left-hand road and Newport ones the right-hand. Except for in the main summer season, June to September most years, when Smallbrook Junction signalbox was opened and the two roads became a conventional double track, splitting into single line routes with a scissors crossover. With single line tokens to collect and issue for two routes, Smallbrook was one of the busiest mechanical junction boxes in the South, especially for such a simple track layout, and its role in smart operating was crucial. The double track was essential for maintaining the full-blown summer timetable on the Ventnor line and it would only take a brief delay on either route at Smallbrook to commence an escalation of late running that would, by mid-afternoon, make the working timetable a work of fiction.

Single or double track, the Ventnor train would sweep through, slowing in summer to collect the token. Now the electrics hurry along the double track to the site of the junction, where a single-line point and protecting sand-drag are controlled from St Johns Road Box. In the

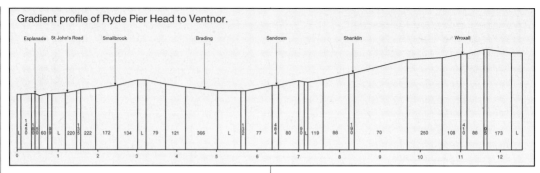

Gradient profile of Ryde Pier Head to Ventnor.

summer, they then slow to a stop at the island's newest station, Smallbrook Junction. A second platform is used by the preserved steam operation of the Isle of Wight Steam Railway and it is proof of the cordial relations that exist between the two lines that the station was built by Network SouthEast and opened as their part of the preserved line's extension in summer 1991 — and NSE was persuaded not to call it 'Smallbrook Interchange'.

From Smallbrook to Brading is the longest unbroken run on the Island Line. The route rises for a mile or so through woodland, to a summit at a low ridge near Rowborough Farm, before descending Brading Bank into the valley of the River East Yar. Crossing farmland, the line finally swings right to approach Brading station.

Brading is now much reduced, with only the former up platform in use. Looking at the graffiti-smothered station, it is hard to believe that less than 10 years ago it was given a major smarten-

up and turned into a community centre for Brading village. Only too clearly, not all the residents appreciated the facility! Across the track, the island down platform and signalbox are abandoned. The former was used by all down trains until 1989, for this was the start of the double track section to Sandown. Installed by the Southern in the 1920s, it was a valuable help in maintaining the tight 'maximum' timetable. When the line was singled, NSE gave much of the lifted track and materials to the IoW Steam Railway at a very generous discount, for use on rebuilding the line from Haven Street to Smallbrook. Without NSE's help, that reopening would probably not have happened.

Until 1953, passengers arriving in the down platform might have seen the Bembridge branch train waiting for them on the other side of the island platform. By then there were few passengers to transfer, so after a brief stop the train would head on southwards.

Bottom left:
The south end of St Johns Road in 1930, by now resignalled for conventional up and down platform operation and with the larger signalbox, second-hand from Waterloo Junction. No 23 *Totland* prepares to leave the down main platform. The two armless dolls on the bracket signal show that it is summer, with double track operation extended to Smallbrook Junction. From autumn to spring, with Smallbrook closed, the arms were replaced and trains were signalled to the Ventnor or Newport lines at St Johns Road. *IAL*

Above right:
No 24 *Calbourne* storms away from St Johns Road with a Ventnor train on 21 June 1961. *R. J. Blenkinsop*

Right:
On a busy summer day, Smallbrook Junction was the most critical point on the whole system for smooth operation. A down train waits for the road as an up train from Ventnor clears the single line. *IAL*

Below:
Brading in pre-Grouping days, with Bembridge (left) and Pier Head trains waiting to depart. *IAL/Bucknall Coll*

Halfway to Sandown is the start of the long climb, with just one brief respite, to the north portal of Ventnor Tunnel. As the gradient profile shows, this line has the longest and most regular grades on the island — a sign of a properly engineered railway with decent earthworks, rather than trying to save money by following the lie of the land. It cost more in the first place but has paid off in better operating conditions ever since. The driver is not forever altering the setting of the controls and the motive power is not shaking itself to bits.

Sandown, once the HQ of the Isle of Wight Railway, is another much reduced station. Once a junction, with the 'Central' line from Newport trailing in from the right to the island platform's outer face, it retains a passing loop, still in regular use and now with automatic points. The signalbox, which once rose improbably through the island platform's canopy roof and later stood alone and

incongruously tall, is therefore no more, another victim of the 1989 changes.

We are now at the northern edge of the island's main holiday resort belt, which the railway skirts on the inland side. There is little to remind us of the past, or the crowds that once passed through here. But until the 1950s, with one of the four hourly Saturday trains each way terminating and commencing here, and with the trains from Newport to reverse as well, it was operationally a hectic place.

The other three trains continued, back on single track now, on varying gradients to Shanklin, an uninterrupted run which the EMUs do not now get. In 1987 a new halt was opened at Lake, (some 50 years after it was first proposed) serving the growing community in what had been a hamlet that held the two resort towns at arm's length. A brief reversal of the prevailing up grade soon ends as the line sweeps gently inland to the rising ground on the edge of Shanklin.

Shanklin station, once a passing point with two platforms and with the buildings on the down side, is now reduced to a single platform with the track ending abruptly at buffer stops, beyond which an underbridge has been removed. The old up track and platform lasted into electric days but were removed, along with the signalbox, as an economy measure, the line becoming in effect a long siding from Sandown. Happily, the handsome buildings mostly remain, looking rather cleaner than they did in later steam days.

Shanklin rather fancied itself as the better of the twin resorts, being larger, with a smarter street plan, a wider beach and a longer pier. It still had a half-mile gap between station and seafront however, and many a weary holidaymaking family, arriving on a Saturday afternoon, must have regretted this. They were, had they known it, better off than their travelling companions going on to Ventnor!

Again, on summer Saturdays, one of the hourly steam services terminated at Shanklin, the other two going on to the terminus. Sweeping west and entering open, rolling farmland, the line hit the most demanding part of the climb to St Boniface Down, the famous Apse Bank, scene of many a photograph. Over a mile of left-hand curve round the foot of St Martin's Down turned the line back to face southwest as Wroxall station was reached.

DOWN TRAINS. SATURDAYS ONLY.	Pass. arr.	Pass. dep.	Pass. arr.	Pass. dep.	Pass. arr.	Pass. dep.	Pass. arr.	Pass. dep.	Pass. arr.	Pass. dep.	arr.	dep.	Pass. arr.	Pass. dep.	Pass. arr.	Pass. dep.	arr.	dep.	Pass. arr.	Pass. dep.
	a.m.	a.m.	a.m.	a.m.	a.m.	a.m.	a.m.	a.m.	a.m.	a.m.			a.m.	a.m.	a.m.	a.m.			a.m.	a.m.
Ryde Pier Head ...	...	8 59	...	9 20	...	9 50	...	10 28	...	10 48	...	...	...	11 5	...	11 25	...	...	...	11 45
„ Esplanade...	9 1	9 3	9 22	9 25	9 52	9 55	10 31	10 33	10 51	10 53	...	...	11 7	11X 9	11 27	11 29	...	...	11 47	11 49
„ St.John's Road	9 6	9 7	9 28	9 30	9 58	10 0	10 36	10 37	10x56	10 58	...	...	11 12	11 17	11 32	11X37	...	...	11 52	11 57
Brading...........	9x15	9 16	9 38	9 40	10 8	10 10	10 45	10 48	11 6	11 8	...	...	11 25	11 28	11 45	11 48	...	...	12 5	12 8
Brading	...	9 18	...	...	...	10 13	...	10 55	...	...	...	...	...	11 34	...	...	...	...	...	12 14
St. Helens.......	9 24	9 24½	...	...	10 19	10 19½	11 1	11 1½	...	...	...	...	11 40	11 40½	...	...	...	...	12 20	12 20½
Bembridge	9 28	...	...	...	10 23	...	11 5	...	...	...	...	...	11 44	...	...	...	...	...	12 24	...
Sandown..........	9 20	9 22	9 44	9 46	10 14	10x16	10 52	10 54	11 12	11 14	...	...	11 32	11 34	11 52	11 54	...	...	12 12	12 14
Shanklin	9 27	9x32	9 51	9x54	10 21	10 23	10x59	11 1	11X19	11 21	...	...	11x39	11 41	11X59	12 1	...	...	12x19	12 21
Wroxall...........	9 40	9x45	10 2	10x 5	10 31	10x33	11x 9	11 11	11X29	11 31	...	...	11 49	11X51	12X 9	12 11	...	...	12x28	12 31
Ventnor	9 50	...	10 10	...	10 38	...	11 16	...	11 36	...	...	...	11 56	...	12 16	...	...	...	12 36	...

DOWN TRAINS. SATURDAYS ONLY.	Pass. arr.	dep.	Pass. arr.	dep.	Pass. arr.	dep.	Pass. arr.	dep.	Pass. arr.	dep.	Pass. arr.	dep.	Pass. arr.	dep.	Pass. arr.	dep.	Pass. arr.	dep.	Pass. arr.	dep.
	p.m.	p.m.	p.m.	p.m.	p.m.	p.m.	p.m.	p.m.	p.m.	p.m.	p.m.	p.m.	p.m.	p.m.	p.m.	p.m.	p.m.	p.m.	p.m.	p.m.
Ryde Pier Head ...	...	12 5	...	12 25	...	12 45	...	1 5	...	1 25	...	1 45	...	2 5	...	2 25	...	2 45	...	3 5
„ Esplanade...	12 7	12 9	12 27	12 29	12 47	12 49	1 7	1 9	1 27	1 29	1 47	1 49	2 7	2 9	2 27	2 29	2 47	2 49	3 7	3 9
„ St.John's Road	12 12	12 17	12 32	12 37	12 52	12 57	1 12	1 17	1 32	1x37	1 52	1 57	2 12	2 17	2 32	2 37	2 52	2 57	3 12	3 17
Brading...........	12 25	12 28	12 45	12 48	1 5	1 8	1 25	1 28	1 45	1 48	2 5	2 8	2 25	2 28	2 45	2 48	3 5	3 8	3 25	3 28
Brading	...	...	...	12 55	...	...	...	...	...	1 55	...	...	...	2 39	...	...	...	3 13	...	...
St. Helens.......	...	...	1 1	1 1½	...	...	2 1	2 1½	...	...	2 45	2 45½	...	...	3 19	3 19½	...	...	...	...
Bembridge	...	...	1 5	...	...	...	2 5	...	...	...	2 49	...	...	...	3 23	...	...	...	...	...
Sandown..........	12 32	12 34	12 52	12 54	1 12	1 14	1 32	1 34	1 52	1 54	2 12	2 14	2 32	2 34	2 52	2 54	3 12	3 14	3 32	3 34
Shanklin	12X39	12 41	12x59	1 1	1x19	1 21	1X39	1 41	1 59	2x 1	2x19	2 21	2X39	2 41	2x59	3 1	3x19	3 21	3x39	3 41
Wroxall...........	12X49	12 51	1x 9	1 11	1 29	1x31	1X49	1 51	2 9	2x11	2 29	2x31	2X49	2 51	3 9	3X11	3 29	3x31	3 49	3x51
Ventnor	12 56	...	1 16	...	1 36	...	1 56	...	2 16	...	2 36	...	2 56	...	3 16	...	3 36	...	3 56	...

Above:
Extract from the SR summer Saturdays working timetable for 1931 (11 July to 19 September).

Left:
With its duty number on the bufferbeam, No 27 *Merstone* heads away from Brading along the double track section to Sandown in June 1964. *J. Goss*

Above right:
Sandown station looking north in 1934, with the Newport platform on the left. The unusual signalbox can be seen rising through the island platform canopy. *LGRP*

Track plan of Sandown.

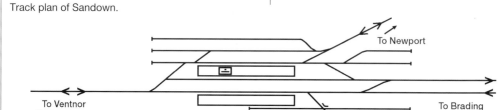

To Newport

To Ventnor

To Brading

Wroxall was a small place, though it has grown in recent years and would probably make better use of a railway than ever before, but in steam days it was quiet enough. On Saturdays it was a regular crossing place and also gave respite to down train loco crews, especially those on a maximum permitted six-coach set, near the 155-ton limit. Less than a mile ahead the view was dominated by the daunting bulk of St Boniface Down but they had barely half that distance to go before plunging into Ventnor Tunnel, 1,316yd long and single track, but happily downhill. Caution was needed though, as the station was entered immediately on leaving the bore, so the run would be taken easily, despite lingering fumes from the last up train.

Ventnor station nestled in a hollow quarried out of the chalk down and the station throat points were literally at the tunnel mouth. Run-round and shunting movements took locos back into the tunnel. The two-track station had a main and island platform, the latter giving two platform faces to one track for no particular good reason, as you could only leave the island platform by passing through a train or using a 'drawbridge', which was run into place when there was no train in the platform or on its way. Otherwise it was isolated.

Originally the tracks ended in a small turntable, just big enough for one of the IWR's Beyer Peacocks, installed to save space rather than for turning locos, which traditionally ran chimney-first from Ryde, where there was no turning facility. The arrival of the longer 'O2s' effectively put it out of business and it was replaced in short order by a conventional run-round spur and points.

Ventnor, the only south-facing resort of any size on the island, also claims the sunniest weather. Our tourists, arriving at the station after a long journey involving quite a wide range of transport experiences, had a moment to appreciate the superb view down over the town to the Channel beyond, before discovering the price they paid for it, a descent of some 200ft to their hotels and boarding houses below. A week later they would have the even less happy experience of struggling back up the same route, just as well laden, at the start of their journey home!

Ventnor was an interesting station, its range of wooden buildings running down the middle of the site, with the station approach on one side and the goods yard on the other. Two long sidings here frequently stored coaching stock, though six-coach sets were rarely berthed intact; the photographers who climbed the hill behind the station have left records which show four coaches per line to have been the common maximum. Like other stations on the line, it was used in winter for stock storage when the demand for coaches fell so dramatically and a handful of four-coach sets on this route and of three-coach ones on the Cowes service was all that was required. Sandown, Brading, St Johns Road and of course Newport, would also fill up with spare stock out of season. But in the summer, when everything that could move was needed, that 12¼-mile run from Ryde Pier Head to Ventnor was a strong contender for the prize of busiest and most intensively worked single line (mostly) in Southern Britain.

Left:
With lost time to make up if possible, No 21 *Sandown* attacks the steep grade out of Sandown with a Ventnor train on 7 June 1965. *J. Goss*

Centre left:
No 17 *Seaview* approaches Shanklin with a Ventnor train on 29 June 1945. The rear vehicle is a full brake/luggage van. *E. R. Wethersett*

Below left:
With safety valves just feathering, No 21 *Sandown* coasts into Shanklin station with a heavy Ventnor train on 16 August 1965. *I. G. Holt*

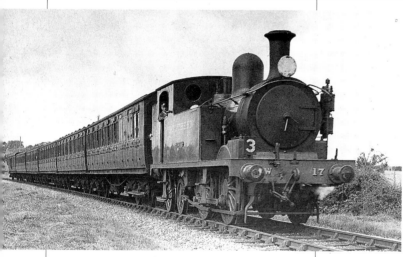

Above right:
Passing through the chalk downland of the southern end of the route, No 28 *Ashey* drifts downhill from Wroxall with a Ventnor-Pier Head train on 30 August 1965. *J. Goss*

Right:
No 18 *Ningwood's* fireman takes the opportunity to bring some coal down while waiting for the token and signal at Wroxall on 28 August 1964. *M. Dunnett*

Everything has gone now, although the location is unmistakable. The railway installation has been replaced by industrial odds and ends, but the caves in the chalk crags are still there and the tunnel mouth is recognisable, though barricaded to keep out straying visitors. Ventnor's tourist trade suffered badly from the loss of the railway, although such little local difficulties caused no loss of sleep among the Ministry of Transport's mandarins. Small wonder that there have been persistent rumours in the town ever since about the rail link being restored in some form or other, though sadly under present circumstances these must realistically be filed under 'wishful thinking'.

Left:
At the top of the climb from Brading, a Ventnor train approaches the north portal of Ventnor Tunnel, still billowing fumes from the last up train to pass through. *M. Dunnett*

Below:
An 'O2' emerges into the light at the south end of the tunnel and immediately enters Ventnor station trackwork. *R. B. Owen*

Above:
Ventnor station from above the tunnel mouth in June 1963, showing clearly the layout of this unusual terminus. No 29 *Alverstone* waits to depart with a Pier Head train. Beyond the station the town (and the road!) falls away steeply to the seafront. *J. Scrace*

Right:
Ventnor in June 1956, showing berthed rakes of coaches and scattered goods wagons, as well as No 29 *Alverstone* ready to depart with a Pier Head train.
Colin Boocock

Right:
End of the line. *Ventnor* stands on the turntable at the end of Ventnor's platforms, taking water while running round in this late pre-Grouping view. The turntable arrangement was made to save space but was replaced by the SR as it was too short for the 'O2s'.
LPC

To Newport and Cowes

The rather longer run from Ryde Pier Head to Newport and Cowes was of a very different character to the Ventnor line. More rural in character and with a more irregular gradient profile, it did however link the island's three main towns. Unfortunately, so did the island's best roads, and competition was inflicting serious damage by the early 1950s.

Part of the problem was that Ryde and Cowes were rival ports for the mainland traffic (to Portsmouth and Southampton respectively) so through traffic was consequently not as great as one might expect. Also neither Newport nor Cowes was a big holiday resort (unless one was into boating or, in an earlier era, royalty-spotting), so even on the peak days, two hourly trains of, often, four coaches sufficed, compared with the Ventnor line's four trains of six coaches. In the winter an hourly service of three coaches more than sufficed and by 1960 the route was losing serious money.

The line closed in February 1966, though goods and engineering trains continued for longer, the latter for nearly another year as electrification equipment was landed at Medina Wharf. Fortunately, nearly half the route survives as the Isle of Wight Steam Railway, so it can still be enjoyed in the obvious way, and parts of the rest survive as public paths. Only in Newport has the railway been totally obliterated, with a thoroughness bordering on the vindictive.

Running from Pier Head, the observant passenger would first notice the difference from the Ventnor service at St Johns Road where, out of the main season, the train took the right-hand track and ran 'wrong road' to Smallbrook, where the junction and the signalbox were closed until next June. Otherwise, in summer, he was quite likely to pass an up Ventnor train at Smallbrook; which train would be 'held' to give way to the other across the junction would be a matter for the signalman's judgement as much as the details of the working timetable.

From Smallbrook the line turned southwest, crossing farmland on a generally rising grade, to Ashey station. Here once there was occasional

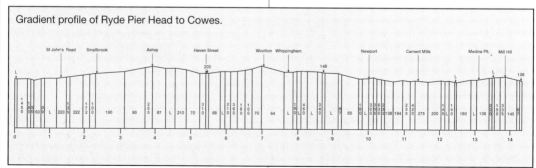

Gradient profile of Ryde Pier Head to Cowes.

Above left:
For its remote location, Ashey had a substantial station building. The loop was out of use by September 1953, when No 35 *Freshwater* was at the former up platform with a Ryde-Cowes train. *J. H. Aston*

Above:
No 18 *Ningwood* is seen at Ashey's replacement platform and shelter on the former down side on 15 May 1965. *Andrew Muckley*

Right:
No 27 *Merstone* heads a Cowes train into Haven Street on 15 May 1965; the unusual design of the SR-rebuilt station is evident. *Andrew Muckley*

Right:
No 33 *Bembridge* arrives at Wootton with a Freshwater-Ryde train on 16 September 1953. *J. H. Aston*

hectic traffic for Ashey Racecourse and a long siding to a local quarry, both long forgotten in the line's last days, though traces of the latter's embankment, curving southwest from the running line, can still be discerned. The station had been a passing point before Havenstreet was upgraded and given a loop in the 1920s (Havenstreet was a more suitable passing point for an even-interval service) and in later years the old up platform, where the main buildings were, was abandoned and the track slewed to the former down platform, when the up platform's foundations began to give trouble. The reopened line uses the down formation, though few passengers use the halt now, and the old station building, a good example of IWCR 'country house' style architecture, survives as a private house.

From Ashey the line curves to run northwest and the gradient soon begins to fall, taking the line into the first of some woodlands that

Left:
The south end of Newport station, with the drawbridge and viaduct visible through the signal bracket. On 17 June 1965 No 24 (its nameplates removed for safe keeping) is running in with a Ryde-Cowes train, while No 21 *Sandown* waits for the road. *M. Dunnett*

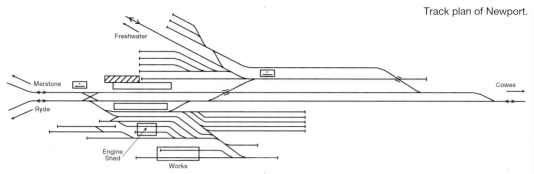

Track plan of Newport.

Freshwater

Merstone

Ryde

Cowes

Engine Shed

Works

Left:
No 18 *Ningwood* makes an impressive departure from Newport as it crosses the former drawbridge over the Medina with a Cowes-Ryde train on 17 June 1965. *M. Dunnett*

Right:
No 27 *Merstone*, with a shield over its Westinghouse pump, has just taken water while waiting to leave Newport for Mill Hill and Cowes on 15 April 1965. *Andrew Muckley*

Below:
Newport after closure; the station in early 1967, its platform roads filled with redundant steam stock awaiting scrapping. Some of the coaches to the right had been reserved for preservation. No trace of the station now remains. *John H. Bird*

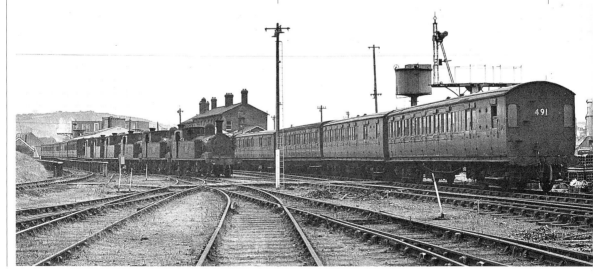

Above:
No 18 *Ningwood* crosses Mill Ponds Viaduct with a Cowes train. *Michael P. Jacobs*

Left:
Medina Wharf was for years the island's main freight terminal. This 1930s scene gives a hint of the scale of the coal traffic and the reason why so many open wagons were needed. *IAL*

accompany it much of the way to Wootton (and once beyond). At the foot of the grade Havenstreet station is reached. Once a single platform with a small yard opposite to serve a local gas works, it was rebuilt in curious style by the Southern. An island platform was provided, with the station building, a real gem of 1920s-style small-scale public transport architecture, at ground level to the north of the running lines. Access to the platforms was and is via a foot crossing.

The original buildings survive in the care of the Isle of Wight Steam Railway, which has made sympathetic additions where necessary, even the large workshop on the south side bearing a passing resemblance to SR practice. Surprisingly, the long-disused gas-house remains too and now houses a souvenir shop and a fine small relics museum. The single-storey extension to the east is a 1970s addition for a station shop, a fact not obvious at first glance, so well has it been matched to the Victorian original. A delightful country station has not wholly lost its character, which is more than can be said for some better-known preserved lines on the mainland!

Climbing now, the line continues through the woods, emerging into open farmland shortly before Wootton; and it is here that the changes begin. Formerly the station (closed in 1953) lay in a cutting just beyond a three-arch overbridge. This cutting, plus the proximity of the main Newport-Ryde road with its more convenient bus service, was the station's undoing. Cut through clay, it became unstable and closure of the station assisted the civil engineer to keep the line open without expensive earthworks. Later it defeated the preservationists too and the reopened line was terminated just short of the overbridge. Bridge and cutting have now been filled in and the steam trains arrive in a simple, one-platform country terminus with a run-round loop and short siding, which captures the flavour of the system's one-time remote outposts — as it was intended to do.

The pre-1966 service ran on westwards, soon reaching — or passing the site of — Whippingham station, another 1953 closure. Built optimistically to serve Queen Victoria's Osborne House over two miles away, it was equally remote from any other source of traffic. How it survived for so long is a mystery. Its passing loop remained in occasional use until 1956, conveniently splitting the long section between Havenstreet and Newport. The station building, another example of IWCR 'country house' architecture, has happily survived as a private house.

From Whippingham the line soon swung left, to parallel the River Medina — and the main road. On the outskirts of Newport it turned to tunnel under this deadly rival and swung through 90° over a viaduct, meeting the line from Merstone on a converging structure. Crossing a drawbridge over the Medina (provided at some expense and much operating inconvenience for the very occasional tall boats which went further upstream), the now parallel lines ran into Newport station.

Newport was in most senses the hub of the Isle of Wight system. Five routes converged there; it was the operating, management and engineering headquarters of the Isle of Wight Central, the kingpin of the island's goods traffic and the largest station on the system. Only in traffic figures was it eclipsed by the one line which did not pass through it; the east coast route from Ryde to Ventnor. The Central's attempts to tap into this traffic with its lines to Sandown and Ventnor, served in the end only to keep it in near-penury, while the IWR almost prospered.

The station possessed an imposing, if somewhat plain, main building, whose long frontage faced intending passengers coming up the station approach. It housed not just the station offices but became the SR's centre of administration, remaining so until the final severe amputations of 1966 rendered adequate the more modest facilities available at Ryde.

There were three platforms, down and up mains plus an up loop. At the north end of the down platform was, until 1953, the bay platform for the Freshwater line. Beyond the platforms were the MPD with its engine shed (closed after the final demise of the 'E1s') and the CME's depot in the former works. North of this, alongside the line to Cowes, was an array of five carriage sidings. The goods yard was behind the down bay.

With its substantial platforms, smart canopies, covered footbridge, two signalboxes and double track seeming at first glance to head off in each direction, Newport station could have played the part of a busy station in many a large regional town. Only on closer study did it reveal itself as the meeting point of a group of single-line branches, for which it would burst into lively activity every so often, before resuming its accustomed slumbers.

Newport had a brief and ghoulish life after death. Following the 21 February 1966 closure, coal trains from Medina Wharf continued to run through, stocking up Ryde MPD with the leftovers of closing depots on the mainland until the place was satiated. The coal concerned was getting pretty knocked about by then; small wonder if the 'O2s' had some steaming problems in their final season. These coal trains were followed by the engineers' trains bringing in supplies for

Right:
Mill Hill station served the south part of Cowes. No 18 *Ningwood* arrives at this pleasant little station with a Cowes train on 18 June 1965.
M. Dunnett

83

Above:
Cowes terminus stood at the foot of a gradient, necessitating a cautious approach. No 29 *Alverstone* runs into the main platform with a train from Pier Head on 9 September 1965. *J. Scrace*

Left:
No 21 *Sandown* running round its train, a 'local' from Newport, in June 1952. After pushing the stock clear of the crossover points, gravity was employed to run the coaches back into the platform, after which the loco would be coupled back on. *N. M. Wyatt*

Left:
Cowes boasted a covered concourse, although its platform canopies were not really adequate to protect arriving passengers from the weather. On 8 July 1964 No 24 *Calbourne* has just arrived with a train from Ryde. *M. J. Howe*

electrification, and later by some demolition trains taking redundant track out. Finally it became the centre for withdrawn stock. Lines of coaches, and eventually the remaining 'O2s', stood in melancholy ruin, awaiting their turn as the scrapmen worked their way methodically through the ranks.

It was even the home for a while for the items purchased for preservation by the Wight Locomotive Society, while negotiations to secure Havenstreet (NB: the railway spelling of this stop varied over the years from 'Haven Street' to 'Havenstreet') proceeded. At last, on 24 January 1971 *Calbourne* worked six coaches and assorted wagons from Newport to their new home, the last trains ever to leave Newport station.

The station building had a brief after-life as the central depot of the island's postal services, ironically a stage in the necessary reorganisation now that rail transport via Ryde Pier Head was no longer a viable operation. More suitable accommodation was soon found and the final fate of the station and indeed all the railway installation at Newport, was total destruction to make way for the Newport bypass road and an adjoining industrial estate.

Back to happier times and our train to Cowes. Leaving Newport, the train passed the carriage sidings and the former Freshwater yard before entering the single line section. It was now running on the oldest railway route on the island, following the west bank of the Medina and never much more than 220yd from the water. Running on undulating but easy grades through open countryside, there were nonetheless some industrial installations which kept the line busy and made Newport the hub of the system's goods traffic.

After easing over the 10mph-restricted, steel girder Mill Ponds Viaduct, the first of these was reached: the cement works, which generated a regular traffic from the chalk quarry at Shide, just south of Newport. Until the works closed after World War 2, it also brought passenger traffic, via a small halt provided mainly for the workforce.

A mile further on and the railway's (indeed the island's) main freight terminal was reached — Medina Wharf. Built by the Central in early days, it was much improved by the Southern and pushed the rival but silt-plagued St Helens into terminal decline. Five sidings plus two wharf roads and two storage loops were provided here, reached by a sharply falling spur from the main line. For years the main regular traffic through the wharf, distributed by rail all over the island, was coal.

We are starting to forget now just how vital coal was to British society before about 1960. Not only did it provide the railway with fuel, it was still the prime heating agent for most homes and businesses. It provided gas too, which most people cooked by, the more advanced used for heating, and a surprising number of places (including some homes, outdated schools and public buildings and a lot of municipal lighting departments) used for illumination. Small wonder that coal traffic on the island was heavy; it goes a long way to explaining those 500 open wagons, many of which could be seen loading at Medina Wharf, or waiting in the sidings to go to the various coal merchants' yards or the gas works sidings.

From Medina Wharf and its halt the line started climbing into Cowes. Mill Hill Halt was reached first, then the short (208yd) Mill Hill Tunnel took the train to the final down grade to Cowes terminus.

Cowes was an elegant station, perched on the hillside a short distance from the Southampton ferry pier. It featured two curved platforms, one with a bay on its outer face, the other backed by a siding. Short canopies led to a glazed-roofed concourse, with a Victorian-classical main building facing the street. Halfway down their length the platforms were crossed by a footbridge, which was there to maintain a public right of way rather than for railway passengers. Under it was a locomotive release crossover, but to use it meant that trains stopped an inconvenient distance from the buffer stops. More common, though apparently not quite given official blessing, was a gravity shunt. The loco would propel the empty train up the grade to clear of that crossover, then drop off, run back and cross to the other track. Once the road was reset, the guard would cautiously run the stock downhill to near the buffer stops, after which the engine would follow it in and couple up. Legend states that on occasions things went wrong and then all hell was let loose!

Nothing remains now; redevelopment has swept it all away as thoroughly as at Newport. You have to go back to Mill Hill station to find clear traces that Cowes once had a railway, and that this was the way in which a respectable (if never as spectacular as at Ryde) number of visitors arrived on the Isle of Wight.

Newport to Freshwater

You have only to look at the gradient profile to see that this was a line built on the cheap. It wriggled across the terrain and if it could not go round a hill it would go over it rather than cut through it. Luckily the gradients were so short (you could expect up to 10 changes per mile) and the train loads so light that small engines were able to do the work. Just as well in the early days, for the permitted axle-load was set so low that the

Left:
FYN No 2 prepares to leave the company's station at Newport in August 1922. Despite it being the height of the holiday season, three coaches clearly sufficed. *IAL/Bucknall Coll*

Centre left:
Having backed its train out of the bay platform, No 35 *Freshwater* heads away from Newport with a Freshwater train on 7 April 1953. Passenger loadings are evidently still light and the train is about to pass the site of the FYN station. *R. J. Buckley*

Below:
For years the only passing point on the Freshwater line, Ningwood was a rather remote location. No 34 *Newport* pauses there with a Freshwater-Ryde train in September 1953. *J. H. Aston*

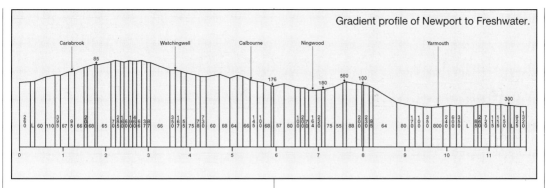

Gradient profile of Newport to Freshwater.

'O2s' were banned from the route until considerable improvements were made in the Southern era.

In its earliest days, the line was likely to be worked by whichever locos the IWCR was brazen enough to send. The 2-2-2 well tanks were favoured before their withdrawal, apparently, being replaced by anything small that was in need of works attention. This was not what the FYN had had in mind when it had entered into an operating agreement with the Central, and helped feed the slow build-up of resentment that led to the 1913 bust-up.

The FYN managed with its two 0-6-0 tanks, though there must have been many nail-biting moments, and the Southern soon despatched the odd redundant IWR Beyer Peacock from Ryde, although nerves must have been taut at times until the civil engineer had improved the light track and weak structures that had caused the Railway Inspectorate such concerns 40 years before, and the 'O2s' could finally reach Freshwater.

From the reversal out of Newport's Freshwater Bay (designated Platform 1 in SR days), the Freshwater train got into its stride on a sharp right-hand curve, passing firstly the remains of that hastily built 1913 station on the left and then the site of the FYN's rudimentary MPD on the right, before climbing to Carisbrooke Halt (nearly 1¼ miles). This served the west suburb of Newport and had potentially the largest traffic flow on the line but the station was inconvenient to reach and with the sparse service, doubtless many locals found it quicker to walk to the shops. Nonetheless it was busy in its day, with tourists visiting nearby Carisbrooke Castle, and until 1927 it possessed a passing loop. It has now effectively vanished.

The line continued to climb until halfway to Watchingwell, when a general falling trend to Ningwood began. Watchingwell (3¾ miles) primarily served a private estate and was remote, so utterly so that the Ordnance Survey of 1934 showed it closed, 19 years before the fact!

Right:
No 29 *Alverstone* leaves Yarmouth for Freshwater in September 1953.
R. C. Riley

Left:
Freshwater in the mid-1920s, with
'Terrier' No 11 waiting to depart on
a Newport train. *IAL*

Below:
No 31 *Chale* runs round at
Freshwater on 3 September 1953,
less than three weeks before
closure. *Ian Pearsall*

The small but pleasing brick station building
survives as a private house.

Another two miles of undulating, curvaceous
descent and the line reached Calbourne, another
station in an almost empty farming landscape,
over a mile from the village that gave it its name.
With one platform plus a back siding, and a
mishmash of little buildings, it had quaintness but
no prosperity. All bar part of the platform has
gone now, swept away for a new cottage. The
train continued downhill to the steel girder
Calbourne Viaduct, over which a 15mph restriction
was in force until the end. A brief but sharp climb
and then downhill again, under a road bridge and
into Ningwood.

Ningwood, nearly seven miles from Newport,
was a passing place until closure, though only

used at busy times; otherwise the small signalbox
was 'switched out' and the line worked as a single
section Newport to Yarmouth (or Freshwater after
Yarmouth loop was removed). The station was at
one end of a straggling road of houses which
clearly brought in little business but supported a
small, brick station house, which has survived as a
cottage, where most other traces of the station
have gone. It gained some tourist traffic as the
'gateway' station to West Wight, thought by many
to be the most scenically attractive part of the
island.

The line was now falling to the coastal levels
and another three miles brought the train to
Yarmouth, the station for the third and smallest of
the island's passenger ports. The foot and vehicle
ferry from Lymington crossed the Solent, as it still

To Newport

does, unaffected by over a century of unrealised plans for a tunnel or a bridge. The station was a brisk quarter-mile from the ferry slipway. Now passengers have less choice; it is bus or car.

Even with the ferry, Yarmouth was not going to generate much traffic for the island's railways, for Lymington is in all honesty remote in mainland port terms; hardly as convenient as Southampton or Portsmouth unless you live west of the New Forest and are travelling specifically to West Wight. However, the ferry has kept in business for a long time, so clearly has its market niche. The station was a small affair, no rival to the other points of entry; built with a passing loop on staggered platforms, it lost this in the 1920s. The platform and its simple building largely survive, with later additions, as public amenities.

From Yarmouth the line swung south to follow the estuary of the River Yar for the final two miles to Freshwater station. The station boasted a single platform, runround loop, small yard, and the most substantial station building on the FYN. Sadly, practically all of it has gone.

Just a little more money and the shareholders of the FYN could have had themselves a far better terminus, for Freshwater was in truth a village at the back of the town. A mile further on was the small but pleasant resort of Totland on its west-facing bay, with Alum Bay close at hand. The development that has filled in the gap between station and sea, and makes the station site seem quite central in an arc of little townships, mostly

post-dates the 1953 closure of the line. It is a great pity, for while it would never have reached anything like the traffic levels of the IWR line, earlier development around Freshwater would have been a boost to the FYN's prosperity. As it was, the Southern certainly did its best. The daily train from Ventnor via Merstone, the 'Tourist', was a popular institution for years (and not just with the enthusiasts who liked the regular use of 'E1' motive power) and actually led to some loops and platforms being lengthened to accommodate it. But there was a limit to what could be done and after traffic levels began to collapse in the late 1940s, the will to be innovative was no longer there. So this curious, marginal railway, built to serve a need that barely existed, succumbed early, though there is some consolation that long sections survive as footpaths.

Newport to Sandown and Ventnor West

Looking at the evidence today, it is hard to say for certain why these two lines were built. Either they were to open up rural areas, or they were an attempt to recoup Cowes's status as the Isle of Wight's main passenger port by providing direct rail links to the main resorts, or they were a pure and simple attempt to rob the IWR of as much of its traffic as possible. The reality probably lies largely in the last two, for the amount of intermediate traffic actually available was sparse indeed.

Though both lines were built nominally independently, the speed with which they came

Right:
Newport station is visible in the left background as a train from Sandown crosses the viaduct behind No 25 *Godshill*.
H. C. Casserley

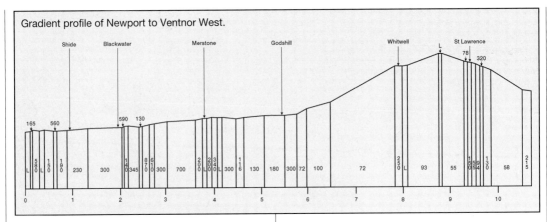

Gradient profile of Newport to Ventnor West.

Left:
Shide, first station out of Newport, served the once-busy chalk quarry, giving some reason for the large building at a minor station, seen here facing towards Merstone. *LPC*

under the IWCR umbrella is instructive. The Sandown line was built by the Isle of Wight (Newport Junction) Railway Co, which was actually formed and commenced construction before the Ryde & Newport line was built, showing the way minds were working in the Cowes and Newport areas. Ruined by the false economies of over-cheap construction, which meant that the Railway Inspectorate demanded expensive extra works before a penny of revenue could be earned, it was soon in liquidation and put firmly into the IWCR camp by the Receiver.

The Newport-Ventnor line's independence was even more nominal and the purpose of cutting into the traffic of the island's sunniest resort even more blatant. Godshill and Whitwell stations were in scattered rural communities, and St Lawrence, where the temporary terminus was opened just beyond the 619yd tunnel through the downs, was a cliffside location that rivalled the Ffestiniog's much later temporary terminus at Dduallt for local traffic potential. Financially exhausted, the railway ended there while the company tried to build up some capital and nerve itself for the 1¼-mile push along the cliffs to the eventual terminus on the very edge of Ventnor, cheekily and misleadingly

named Ventnor Town until the SR knocked some sense into things.

Needing extra rolling stock (and in the case of Ventnor, reasonably competent locomotives) to work the services, the two lines were to be a drain, rather than a benefit, on the Central's coffers, contributing to the dire straits of the company. It might have done quite well, had it been content with just a Cowes to Ryde line but these two branches, plus of course, stocking and working the FYN, put extra demands on its stock department that could only be met by buying other railways' cast-offs at knock-down prices.

From Newport to the junction at Merstone (3¾ miles), the line climbed steadily, following the valleys of the Medina then one of its tributaries. Leaving Newport station over the drawbridge and then the southern of the two diverging viaducts, it skirted the town to reach Shide and its chalk pit, three-quarters of a mile from the junction. The chalk pit kept up a healthy traffic to the cement works north of Newport for many years. This was in fact the last part of the IW(NJ)R to open, some 10 years after work began at the Sandown end, to such poverty was the company reduced by its problems with the

Right:
Merstone, seen here from the Newport end, was surely the last word in simple junction stations. In this 1930 view, Mr MacLeod is standing by the signalpost while on a tour of his domain. *LPC*

Above:
Passenger access to Merstone platform was from the level crossing at the south end. Beyond this crossing, the two tracks parted company for their different destinations with a simple runround/crossover connection. In September 1952, shortly before closure of the Ventnor West line, No 27 *Merstone* waits, left, with a Sandown train, while No 35 *Freshwater* is ready to leave for Ventnor West. *H. C. Casserley*

Right:
Merstone seen from the level crossing, after closure of the Newport-Sandown line in 1956. *I. P. Russell*

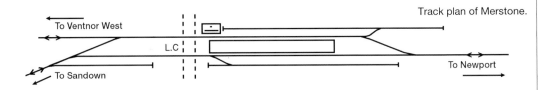

Track plan of Merstone.

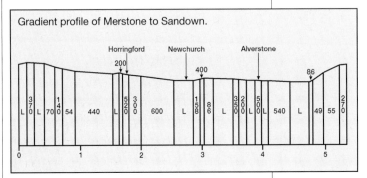

Gradient profile of Merstone to Sandown.

Below:
A Sandown-Newport train runs into
Horringford behind No 25 *Godshill*
in August 1953. *A. W. Burges*

Inspectorate. Equally, the section has now been
largely obliterated by road and drainage works and
other changes to the urban scene, no clear
evidence of a railway existing until just south of
Shide, where the old trackbed reappears as a
footpath.

From Shide the line ran southwards alongside
the Medina for a mile or so, before the valley
opened out at Blackwater station. This was a
simple affair (though with a pleasing staff cottage,
which survives) as befitted its remote location; a
single platform with a timber building, and a back

siding. Swinging southeast, the line followed the
widening but still barely populated valley another
mile and three-quarters to Merstone.

If ever a model were wanted for a basic rural
junction, Merstone would be a near perfect
candidate. It stood half a mile from the hamlet that
gave it its name and a good deal further from
anywhere else. The layout was delightful in its
simplicity; the Sandown line took the form of a
loop with an island platform, on which stood a
canopied building. Just north of the point where
the arms of the loop rejoined, the Ventnor line

Above:
Newchurch was one of the island's most basic stations, despite which it still had a signal cabin inside the station building. Photographed here facing Sandown, just before closure in 1956. *M. E. Ware*

Below:
IWC No 4 tops the final 1 in 54 climb into Sandown station with a train from Cowes circa 1920. *LPC*

turned out of the western track. Outside each loop line was a siding and headshunt.

Ventnor trains could obviously only use the west loop and platform face and the convention was that Sandown trains in either direction used the other side as a rule. On occasions when Sandown line trains crossed here, if the Ventnor train was present it was tucked out of the way into the west headshunt, emerging once the coast was clear, and after a quarter-hour of unwonted activity the whole place would soon settle down to its more typical placidity.

Sadly, barely a trace remains of this real little gem of rural railway practice of an earlier age.

Falling now after the steady climb from Newport, the Sandown line swung left through almost 90°, to run northeast and then generally eastward along the East Yar Valley. The line passed through three simple, one-platform stations, roughly a mile apart: Horringford, Newchurch and Alverstone. Each served a scattered rural community and possessed a siding, rarely used indeed in latter days. Horringford and Alverstone boasted neat, rendered-brick buildings; Newchurch had to make do with little more than a hut.

Finally the line left the Yar Valley floor with another great sweeping curve, right-hand this time, and climbed up to Sandown station, running in at the back of the island platform, just over eight miles from Newport. Had the line met its original expectations in time, this would have been convenient for passengers using it for Cowes-Ryde trips, although a cynic would suggest that even then the short sea journey between the two might well have been quicker. As it was, the route was condemned to be of minor importance, though in the Southern era it did make a useful contribution to the business of moving visitors round the island by train, a trade which MacLeod and his successors pursued with much vigour and some success.

Meanwhile, a train leaving Merstone on the Ventnor West line faced the prospect of a constant climb through even more remote surroundings as it followed the upper Yar towards its source, without the opportunity of a junction for exchange traffic at the end. Small wonder that the line was the island's first casualty, on 15 September 1952,

a year before the Freshwater line succumbed. Much of the flavour of a trip on the line can happily be recalled at the IoW Steam Railway, when at quiet times an amazing little triumph of restoration can be seen, a genuine Ventnor West train. For much of the year a two-coach push-pull set sufficed and in the 1920s this need was met by a pair of ex-LCDR four-wheelers, converted to saloons with a driving cab at the end of one coach. On withdrawal both coaches were sold as sheds and remarkably both survived into the 1980s, when the IoWSR was able to buy them. Fitted onto suitable underframes, totally and beautifully restored, they can sometimes be seen running with a 'Terrier' as they did so often on the Ventnor West run more than half a century ago. That such a minute train could cope with the demands of the line speaks volumes.

There were two stations before the 619yd St Lawrence Tunnel, second longest on the island. Godshill was a single platform, reduced to an unstaffed halt some time before closure, although the substantial buildings survive in private use. Whitwell was somewhat grander, with a passing loop, although this saw little serious use in its life. Again, the buildings still provide a clear link with the past.

After a quite demanding final climb, featuring over a mile of 1 in 72 and then a three-quarter

Above left:
In wartime black livery, No 8 *Freshwater* leaves Merstone with a Ventnor West train in June 1945. *IAL*

Left:
On 13 September 1952, the final day of the Ventnor West line, No 27 *Merstone* carries a commemorative headboard as it crosses the upper Yar valley on the early stages of the run to Ventnor. *Pamlin Prints*

Right:
St Lawrence station from the west in early SR days, with both track and station undergoing much-needed maintenance. This was the terminus of the line for its first three years. *LPC*

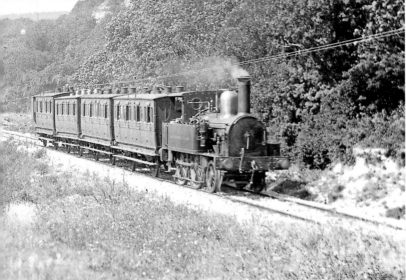

Left:
An IWC train headed by No 5 scuttles downhill along the Undercliff section between St Lawrence and Ventnor Town, not long after opening. *LGRP*

Below:
Ventnor West, looking towards the buffer-stops, in the early 1930s. *IAL*

Left:
Ventnor West had much of the flavour of a rural terminus. This 1934 view of the station throat shows that the trackwork had been simplified since the previous scene had been photographed, also that the signalbox nameboard had been updated by removing the raised-letter 'Town' and painting 'West' in its place. *LGRP*

mile of 1 in 93, the line levelled and then began falling as it entered the tunnel, just a mile from Whitwell. Running steeply downhill through the bore, the line curved eastward just before emerging onto its cliff-ledge location and running into the basic, single-platform St Lawrence station.

This was the terminus of the line for three years, from July 1897 until the line was completed to Ventnor in June 1900; the choice of such a terminus being forced on the company by the need to regain a little financial strength after the costs of getting so far. Certainly it was far from an ideal location, with few local residents and over two miles from Ventnor. That town, or rather its western fringe, was finally reached when the 1¼

miles along the none-too-stable Undercliff was completed and the railway reached its pleasing little two-platform terminus with its small goods yard. Sadly, neither were ever to see overmuch use; goods customers preferred the competing IWR's more central facilities (although a fair amount of coal traffic from Medina Wharf gave the branch stability for some years), as did most passengers. It is doubtful whether the second platform was ever seriously needed. That location on the very fringe of the town was a millstone round the line's neck, however delightful to the enthusiast the terminus might be. Happily the main building has managed to survive in private use, though nearly all other vestiges of the station have vanished beneath redevelopment.

Right:
'O2' No 14 *Fishbourne* brings a Bembridge train round the branch's final curve on the approach to Brading on 13 July 1952. The junction signals and Brading signalbox are in the left background. *A. Robson*

Below:
St Helens Harbour was a busy commercial port for many years. This 1930 view shows a healthy number of railway wagons along the right-hand quay. *LPC*

Brading to Bembridge

The Bembridge branch was, not surprisingly, another early casualty, closing in September 1953. Its origins were more involved however, as it began in the earliest days of the IWR as a short spur to Brading Harbour. The development of St Helens as a commercial wharf and flood protection works saw the end of the ancient port and the line was extended to the new facility and the village of Bembridge beyond.

For most of its early career the line was the preserve of the IWR's 'odd loco out', the Manning Wardle 0-6-0ST *Bembridge*. The ex-Golden Valley coaches, among the few six-wheelers to work on the island, were its regular companions in Edwardian days. *Bembridge* had an unlikely fate. It was requisitioned for military service in World War 1 but never went to the Continent; instead it served the military railways of Southern England, being scrapped in the 1920s. The Bembridge branch meanwhile, fell to the care of the 2-4-0Ts, until the line was upgraded to take the 'O2s'.

The 2¾-mile branch was almost level, featuring just two stations, both surprisingly substantial. St Helens has survived, largely recognisable although its surroundings have radically changed. Bembridge terminus by contrast has vanished, a victim of the commercial redevelopment that followed Bembridge's rise as a smart sailing harbour. One other feature at Bembridge was the turntable in lieu of a runround spur and points, a similar arrangement to Ventnor's. In this case however, it lasted until the end, for there was no room to change it for more conventional arrangements. However, it was renewed in early SR days, the original which could just cope with the Beyer Peacocks being replaced with one just big enough for the 'O2s'.

St Helens was a lively commercial port for half a century, until the SR's rebuilding of Medina Wharf eclipsed it, and its quays were served by a network of sidings. A good part of the island's pre-Grouping stock arrived by this route, including *Bonchurch*, whose arrival included a more intimate acquaintance with the sea than had been intended — surely one of the most unusual introductions to traffic that any railway has ever arranged for a new locomotive!

Below:
Bembridge in Edwardian days, showing the three ex-Golden Valley Railway coaches behind *Ryde*, ready to leave for Brading. The passenger coaches are six-wheelers, the middle axles having generous sideplay.
LPC

The Electric Era

Portrait of the Isle of Wight Railways

Whether or not BR saw the electrification of the remaining line as a short-term sop before it could be closed and forgotten, there is no doubt that it took the conversion seriously once the bit was forced between its teeth. The major rebuild of Ryde pier, the provision of sub-stations, general improvements of the infrastructure and other works were all signs of giving a neglected little system a shot in the arm.

Having accepted that redundant London Underground stock was the only affordable option, BR bought a batch of ex-Tube stock for conversion. It is only fair to the memory of that stock to say that it was not being retired early but after a long, hard life earning its keep charging to and fro beneath the

capital. It was in every sense due for replacement and it is a point to ponder that while a batch of these cars went to operate the Island Line, another was despatched to the Science Museum!

BR was to send 45 electric coaches to the island, arranged in four-car and three-car sets, with

Below:
With a van acting as a match truck to link otherwise incompatible coupling and buffering designs, No 24 *Calbourne* takes one of the first-delivered electric cars on a test/inspection run for Ministry of Transport inspectors on 25 September 1966. The special is seen near St Johns Road. *R. Tunstall*

the capability of running as seven-car units for maximum flexibility. Initial conversion work included a change from four-rail to three-rail current supply and the removal of some seating for extra luggage space. This was after all still the era when summer Saturday crowds arrived at Pier Head for transport to Shanklin.

The stock was disposed into six four-car and seven three-car sets, Nos 041-046 and 031-037, designated 4-VEC and 3-TIS units ('Vectis' was the Latin name for the island). Painted Rail Blue, they began the new service in time for Easter 1967, after a three-month shut-down that

Left:
A posed publicity shot inside one of the new coaches, released in January 1967, shows the open, airy environment, the ample luggage space — and a mainland coach through the window! *British Railways*

Below:
Shanklin in March 1974. The service train is at the former down platform; the other track accommodates stock stored awaiting the increased demands of the summer service. The up platform and signalbox are still intact. *R. E. Ruffell*

One other power unit sent to the island was Hunslet 0-6-0 diesel shunter No 2554 for engineering service. Seen with some surviving wagons at St Johns Road in 1974. *J. Scrace*

followed the end of steam on 31 December 1966.

The electric stock was welcomed by the people it served, whatever the enthusiasts might have thought, and certainly the interiors had an airy brightness about them that belonged to that era, rather than the wood-panelled compartments of a previous age. An increase in line speed from 40mph to 45mph allowed smart running and an improvement on overall schedules which made the line more attractive than it had been for years.

Sadly, things were not to stay so favourable. The island's holiday trade was changing and the traditional week-long break was in decline. As the 22-year rule of the 'Vectis' stock ran on, passenger figures were falling. In one respect this was a blessing, for as the units gave ever-more-fundamental troubles to the engineers at Ryde, the solution was to take some stock out of traffic and cannibalise it.

Meanwhile the Rail Blue livery, an unfortunate corporate identity colour if ever there was one, was wearing even worse in the island's marine atmosphere than on the mainland. Uninspired deep blue soon faded to drab, dreary, chalky blue. The island trains began to look seriously uncared for, which was an insult to the dedicated team at Ryde Works, who continued their tradition of ingenuity in keeping a fleet of other people's cast-offs in the best possible condition. In due course the fleet was repainted into standard blue and grey, which smartened things up for a while. But it did not cure the underlying problem; the fleet was wearing out.

Thus a somewhat depleted fleet lasted into the late 1980s, although by then its once-fresh look had long since faded. Rough riding, accompanied by constant and alarming rattles, are the principal memories of passengers from the 1980s.

This was largely countered by an imaginative local management, which introduced a 20min frequency service. Frequent short trains went a long way to retaining the available business and indeed to building up new trade. The formation of Network SouthEast was a blessing for the line, bringing as it did a new and aggressive attitude to survival by growth where possible, rather than simply existing in the hope that something might happen. New paint on stock and stations might have only covered over the underlying problems but in so doing it brought new heart to the operation. The opening of Lake station, the first new station on the island since Edwardian times, was another encouraging sign, as was a director who saw the steam railway as a potential ally rather than an irrelevance.

The high point in the Island Line's recent history was the arrival of new stock in 1989. Somehow, this event eclipsed the considerable rationalisation that accompanied it. To take the 'down side' first, the use of the old down track on Ryde Pier virtually ceased; the Brading-Sandown double track section was singled, Brading and Sandown signalboxes were closed and St Johns Road Box took control of the entire line. The passing loop at Sandown was worked by automatic points and Sandown to Shanklin remained as virtually a long passenger siding.

However, new trains were new trains, and they looked considerably more modern than the first generation of electrics. Once inside, their origin was evident — London Underground again.

The same reason prevailed, of course; nowhere else was stock of a suitably small size available at a price which this heavily subsidised line could justify. This time the choice was for 16 cars of 1938 stock, being taken out of traffic after a long and honourable career. More importantly, the conversion was much more thorough. Eastleigh Works gave the stock a major refurbishment and it entered service on the island immaculate, and surprisingly modern-looking, in NSE livery, to the trumpet-blowing that the Network was so skilled at arranging to upgrade even the most prosaic event! Meanwhile the poor, tired old 1924 stock staggered thankfully off to oblivion. Plans to keep a set as an 'official' preservation venture did not materialise.

That a line which in 1966 was seen as needing over 40 vehicles was in 1989 given just 16, and that without lots of luggage space, is instructive in how business on the Island Line had declined in the intervening years. But looking objectively, what has happened is that the holiday peaks have collapsed. The core business, though reduced, was holding up and being developed and the line looked set for a healthy future, based on some real stability at last.

Following privatisation, it is too soon yet to say how things will develop. The uniqueness of the line's position was recognised in that it was privatised as an entire unit, rather than on the multi-layered approach of the main system. That it did not go to the local consortium which bid, however, but became another satellite of the Stagecoach empire, suggests that some lessons have still to be learned.

A visit to the line in late 1997 showed that the optimism of the late 1980s was still there in part. However, the 20min interval service had gone,

replaced by an uneven (and therefore annoying) two services per hour on a 20min, 40min interval basis. Worse still, there was the odd one-hour gap without trains at all, which considerably reduced the attractiveness of the railway as a quick and easy way of getting about on the east coast of the island. All in the interests of economy no doubt, but it does seem that some of the lessons of the past have been rather hastily forgotten in the interests of a tidy balance sheet.

Below:
In July 1977, a seven-car down train crosses from the old up to the down line after calling at Ryde Esplanade and accelerates down the ramp to Esplanade Tunnel. The track on the pier is effectively two long sidings, necessitating such a manoeuvre at Esplanade. *M. Hall*

Above right:
By now repainted in an island version of standard BR blue and grey, a seven-car train pulls out of Esplanade for Shanklin on 14 June 1982. *Brian Morrison*

Below right:
In 1989 the ageing VecTis sets were replaced with eight two-car sets of LT 1938 stock. Unit 483006 enters Sandown from Ryde on 4 May 1992, passing the permanent way yard. The fleet of engineers' wagons is now more up to date and the large pile of ballast is for improving the track; previously shingle ballast had been the norm — and part of the reason for the speed limit. *Chris Wilson*

Left:
Calbourne arrives at a crowded Haven Street on 24 January 1971, with the final train from Newport; the preserved railway was officially 'moving in' at Haven Street and moving its rescued stock from the doomed Newport station site.
Dr J. Mackett

Left:
By Whit Monday 1971 the railway was able to offer a short push-pull trip in the direction of Wootton. *Calbourne* is ready to leave on another journey. The 'O2' was facing Ryde at this time, a result of being transferred from St Johns Road to Newport by road in 1967 and being unloaded the wrong way round. *John H. Bird*

Below:
Smallbrook Junction station, from the up end of the Steam Railway platform, in October 1997, with an Island Line train departing for Ryde. Built by NSE to give cross-platform interchange between the two lines, the station is used by Island Line trains whenever the Steam Railway is operating.

The Preserved line

While the 'official' line on the Isle of Wight is now little more than the first-opened section of the Isle of Wight Railway of 1864, there is happily a thriving preserved section of the old system. In mileage terms not so much shorter now than the Island Line, the Isle of Wight Steam Railway operates the five-mile section from Smallbrook Junction to Wootton.

It does so in an authentic style that no other standard gauge preserved railway in Britain can match. All of its coaches and three of its four regular passenger locomotives have impeccable Isle of Wight pedigrees; its trains always consist of coaches which worked on the system before 1966 and the chances are that the locomotive did so too. No other standard gauge line can even touch this originality.

The reasons are simple; this is what the railway was set up to do and it has so far resisted the temptation to import 'strange' stock, although it succumbed in one direction during 1997. After all, the old problem still applies — nearly all alternative sources of stock simply will not fit.

The railway and its supporting society grew out of the feeling in the early 1960s that the island's system was somehow special. From the failure of early hopes to keep things as they were, the Wight Locomotive Society was formed, the direct predecessor of the present organisation. The intention then was to preserve a set of coaches and hopefully an 'O2' for static display on the island as a reminder of the past. Plans soon focussed on a location somewhere on the Ryde-Newport section. At the time of closure there was a strong possibility that this would reopen as an early light rail scheme. Saddler Vectrail planned to take it over and run light railcars on the route. For various reasons the attempt failed. The society had to rethink.

By this time, the WLA had purchased five coaches and, thanks to the generosity of the artist David Shepherd, had secured an 'O2'. No 24 *Calbourne* was the choice, as one of those in best condition in 1966. The stock was stored with the other withdrawn items at Newport until 1971; early in the year the association finally secured a

lease on Haven Street, *Calbourne* was steamed and worked the last ever trains from Newport station on 24 January. The five coaches, plus another donated to the association, various goods stock items and an assortment of spares were worked to their new home, just days before demolition of the rest of the line commenced.

Looking back, it seems incredible that after so much enthusiast attention in the mid-1960s, only one loco and six coaches could be saved out of such a large fleet. Over a dozen pre-Grouping locomotives, complete and in working order, more than 50 historic carriages; and only a token selection saved. But these were the early days of standard gauge preservation; in 1966 only the Bluebell and Middleton Railways were operating, the money and the manpower of later years were simply not there. Most enthusiasts soon forgot about the island as they became engrossed in the 1967 rundown of steam on the South Western main line. The Bluebell Railway did in fact consider buying some stock from the island but the cost of hiring the floating crane to bring it back over Spithead made the venture impossibly expensive.

How different things would be in 10 years' time; but meanwhile the small group of preservationists who were to form the Isle of Wight Steam Railway pressed on with their plans — and all credit to them for daring to do so.

The original static display concept was soon ditched in favour of a working line and an operation eastward towards Wootton was commenced, although it was more than a decade before the station there was open, and that was a new one to the east of the road bridge, the unstable cutting beyond being filled in.

Meanwhile not only was Havenstreet being developed with the familiar features of a preserved line's headquarters but the hunt was on for further suitable stock. The luckiest break of all was the securing of two 'Terriers' which had worked on the island; No W11 *Newport*, which was one of a threesome that Butlins bought in 1964, and No W8 *Freshwater*, that returned to the island after a sojourn on display outside the 'Hayling Billy' public house on Hayling Island!

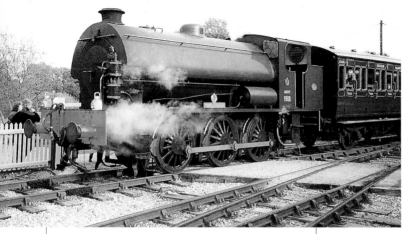

Left:
A valuable addition to the steam fleet, Hunslet 'Austerity' No 198 *Royal Engineer* is on loan from the Army, the most modern steam engine yet to work on the island. It is arriving at Haven Street from Smallbrook Junction in October 1997. The first coach is the newly-restored ex LBSC four-wheeler No 2343.

Centre left:
Stopped for boiler repairs, *Calbourne* stands on show at Haven Street, with a thermometer chart showing progress in fund raising. At its last major overhaul, completed in 1995, the 'O2' was returned to SR livery and given an original-style bunker.

Below right:
The SR's Haven Street station building and platform survive, joined by a sympathetically designed catering hall. Less 'period' buildings are set back behind the trees. Otherwise the only major change to the station scene is the appearance of fences, deemed necessary to help manage the crowds now using this once-quiet station.

Both have been restored to traffic and play an essential role in keeping the line running.

On the coaching front, an additional bogie coach has been secured, an ex-Brighton third, not from the island fleet but identical to some which were sent; it is being restored at the time of writing. But the true glory of the line is in its growing fleet of operational four-wheelers. These owe their existence to the fact that the Southern Railway sold off many bodies of redundant stock for use as outhouses, holiday homes and so on. Over the past 20 years the railway has been buying back some of the best survivors and has plans to retrieve some others, to meet its goal of presenting as wide a range as possible of types of vehicle that once ran on the system.

To date four four-wheelers have been returned to traffic; one ex-North London Railway, one ex-Brighton, and the real gem — the ex-LCDR pair that formed the Ventnor West line push-pull train for some years, Set No 484. All have been superbly refurbished inside and out and mounted on the adapted chassis of SR parcels vans.

Just as much hard work has been expended on the bogie fleet but there the results are less spectacular to the casual viewer. This is largely because the stock is needed in service for as much of the time as possible and total rebuilds are as yet a luxury to be dreamed of. Improvements take place almost unobtrusively, mixed in with what is in all honesty the greater achievement — keeping these elderly coaches in service and arresting the deterioration which otherwise would have had them fall to pieces years ago!

Perhaps the greatest achievement of the IoWSR has been the 'backroom' one of winning acceptance at an official level. From being seen as almost an irrelevance in the 1960s, it is now recognised as an important member of the island's tourist industry; as such it is well regarded by the Island Council and other bodies, including the ferry companies. Its relationships with

Network SouthEast were excellent and it is on cordial terms with the new operators of the Island Line.

One result of this rising status was the extending of the line eastward from Haven Street through Ashey to Smallbrook and the opening of this section in 1991. A long-held dream of the railway, it would have been achieved anyway but it all happened much faster than was at first expected, due to the level of support given. Crucial was NSE, which not only supplied the track materials from the lifted second track on the Brading-Sandown section, but also built the new joint station at Smallbrook Junction. One of the most remote stations on the former BR network (it does not even have footpath access), Island Line trains stop there whenever the Steam Railway is operating.

This has not been the end of the progress of the project by any means. An important step was the arrival of the 'Austerity' 0-6-0ST *Royal Engineer* on long-term loan from the military; not a typical island engine by any means (though a linear successor to the Manning Wardles), it has been an essential part of the fleet with 'Terrier' No 8 out of traffic and *Calbourne* suffering a repeat of boiler trouble. Further carriages are in the pipeline, not only an LBSC bogie third identical to some that ran on the island to add an extra bogie coach to the fleet, but several more coach bodies awaiting restoration to add to the representative pre-1935 stock. The agreement to bring the two Ivatt 2-6-2Ts from Quinton Road to the island will take the load off the ageing original locos in the most appropriate way possible, bringing to reality the plan for this class's younger sisters to work on the lines in the early 1960s. The only truly authentic

alternative way of bringing the motive power fleet up to the necessary level would be the construction of a replica 'O2' or so, with all the remaining 'Terriers' and the sole surviving 'E1' firmly spoken for.

The railway's expansion in the future must surely be constrained by its ability to carry potential passengers. Expansion of the working fleet to meet growing demand is more problematical here, where the usual mainland solution of buying a few Mk 1 coaches is out of the question. So a slow but steady increase as further vintage stock becomes available seems the most likely option.

The biggest challenge of all lies to the west of Wootton station. Since the reopening to Smallbrook, the possibility of reopening towards Newport has been a subject for discussion, not just on the railway but between it and other bodies. It is all low-level so far but the subject will not lie down. Short of a funding miracle there is no real likelihood of returning to Newport station itself but certainly a new station on the east bank of the Medina is physically possible. It will take years, money and hard work, to say nothing of building up the working fleet to cope with the increase in passenger miles; but it remains a real possibility for some time in the future.

The Isle of Wight Steam Railway remains one of the smaller players on the preservation scene but it is one of the most energetic, one of the friendliest and thanks to its unique philosophy, one of the most authentic. It is playing an essential role in keeping alive the spirit and flavour of the old Isle of Wight Railways as they were known and loved for the first two-thirds of this century. Long may it continue to do so.

Envoi

Memories of the 1930s and SR Plans by Dr R. F. Youell

Talk of the Isle of Wight Railways awakens some of my happiest memories.

It is a great pity that so much of the system was wiped out before the preservation movement began to turn the tide, and did it so well. All the more credit to the IoWSR staff for their efforts.

Readers might be interested in a proposal which, largely due to the last war, never materialised.

Not all users or railway enthusiasts recall just how good the steam-operated services on the island were. I spent many of my summer holidays at Sandown in the 1930s and purely by chance the boarding house manageress's husband was the Stationmaster, Mr A. Wheway. I spent most of the holidays in Sandown signalbox, rather than admiring the Needles, Alum Bay or Blackgang Chine, among the many delights the Isle has to offer tourists.

It was fascinating to find that the train service was uncannily like the famous 'Jazz' service of my native Great Eastern. Many of the SR's steam services in the London suburbs were by contrast the target of hostile remarks from the customers. There the overcrowding and general scruffiness were made a thing of the past by the legendary achievements of the Southern Electric.

The GER had worked out that a properly organised steam service could achieve almost as much as electrification. The same principles of organisation and timing to the second worked just as well on the Isle of Wight. A combination of rolling stock and locos from the pre-Grouping constituents of the Southern were turned into an efficient service. Westinghouse brakes (as on the

Left:
A seven-car train approaches Shanklin in August 1983. The wide formation is evident on the left side; this would have given the SR the room to extend the double track section south from Sandown to Shanklin. *Alex Dasi-Sutton*

GER) facilitated rapid turn-round, sharp braking and quick release.

Sandown of course was a kind of miniature Clapham Junction. In the peak summer season, as many trains as possible were fitted into the main line from Ryde Pier to Ventnor. Many of them were first stop Sandown. Some were advertised as first stop Shanklin but usually stopped at Sandown merely to pick up the staff for the single line. The combination of Ventnor, Shanklin, Sandown and all-stations trains was run on a pretty good approximation to a regular interval service.

Sandown to Brading was run on ordinary block working, being double track. The single line to Shanklin was run by electric train staff, so that if need be two trains could follow each other in the same direction.

Most of the other trains at the junction started there and were all stations to Newport, with through runs to Cowes, the Freshwater line or Ventnor West. There was an exception in the crack train of the day — the 'Tourist' or the 'Freshwater Flyer'. This ran from Ventnor to Freshwater, with several nonstop sections. The late F. A. Long, a native of Wight, recalled some of the speeds achieved by the nonstops. The performance resembled that of the tiny 'J69s' on the GER, simply hurtling along with their 'First Stop Walthamstow' rush hour expresses from Liverpool Street. True the Vectis trains were not as long but pro rata the achievement and appearance were as good.

The size of Ryde Pier Head station and the cramped space between the buffers and tunnel mouth at Ventnor set a limit to the length of trains that could be run, so the operators made up in frequency what they could not achieve by lengthening trains. One had to come down 'at the double' from the box to the platform at Sandown to exchange single line staffs, or the tablet and pouch that controlled the Newport line as far as Merstone Junction.

Nothing seemed to go wrong and an atmosphere of quiet efficiency seemed to keep things running perfectly and on time. Yet just as on the 'Jazz' service with its 2min headway, on

Left:
Pier Head in 1927, the last year of electric operation on the tramway. A tram is on its way to Esplanade station, about to pass the fine bracket signal controlling entrance to Pier Head station's platforms. *O. J. Morris*

Right:
An undated view of the tramway in BR days. A tram and trailer head south, past an impressive queue of passengers waiting for the ferry to Portsmouth. *IAL*

the island punctual running meant to seconds rather than to minutes. The double track section to Brading provided a long passing section to give a small recovery time for trains affected by the 'bottleneck' between Smallbrook Junction and Brading. Timing trains meant really snappy work, as the single line section to Shanklin started not far from the end of Sandown platforms and trains from Shanklin could not be held up by a shunting movement right in front of them.

There is a limit to the traffic that can be carried on any intensively used line. The Southern Electric had to put in a flyover at Wimbledon to deal with difficulties. The GER planned a flyover between London and Stratford to increase the frequency of trains to Gidea Park, a sort of pre-Grouping ghost that materialised in 1948 at Aldersbrook instead. No-one was more forward-looking than the Southern at attracting more passengers. I am indebted to the late Mr Wheway, who gave me details of improvements that had been approved by the SR for the Isle of Wight.

The SR already had a stretch of land wide enough to double the track from Sandown to Shanklin, with a new station halfway to serve a busy area of population. In this way the risk of delays on the single line would be eliminated. More trains could be run to terminate at Shanklin, with a bay platform to avoid blocking the main line, as happened at Sandown, plus the ability to run more of the Newport trains to and from there instead of Sandown. The awkward problem was that the width of land owned by the SR north of Brading was not enough to double the track from there to Smallbrook. Negotiations were in hand in the 1930s for the purchase of land to enable this widening to

be carried out, which would have given double track throughout from Ryde Pier Head to Shanklin.

Readers will be aware that in the winter season the line from St Johns Road to Smallbrook was run as a 'double single' section but in summer, with Smallbrook Junction Box open, this section became a key point in the efficiency of the whole service. The result of the planned improvements would have been room for more trains in the summer peak but, probably more important, the fact that one train running late would no longer start a chain reaction of difficulty on the single line sections. The fact that such problems were very rare was due to skilful operation, and the increasing passenger figures meant that widening was by then a necessity.

Regrettably World War 2 broke out just before the plan came to fruition and the shovels were never used to mark the start of the new work. Without criticising BR and now Stagecoach for the electric service, one can only wonder just how good the railways of Wight would have been, had the widening been accomplished.

Please excuse my frequent reference to the GER. However, to say that the Vectis steam services of the 1930s were as well organised as the 'Jazz' service is in fact the highest praise I can give.

Finally, my thanks to the preservation people for their good work — it is a great pity that demolition over the years has made it almost impossible to think in terms of aiming at Newport, the capital of the island, as the eventual terminus.'

Fred Youell
Founder & President, Middleton Railway Trust

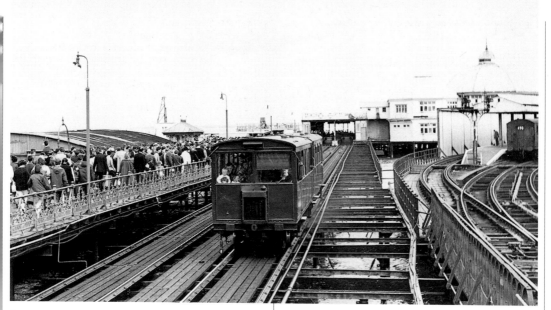

Ryde Pier Tramway

Mention of the tramway on Ryde Pier has been made at times in this portrait. A few words more seem appropriate.

The tramway first opened, horse-drawn, in 1864, running on a structure immediately to the east of the foot-pier. It was extended through Ryde to link the ferry with St Johns Road station in 1871. The opening of the joint LBSC/LSWR line to the pierhead soon saw the end of this extension but the pier tramway settled down to live with its new neighbour, mainly carrying passengers for Ryde who were discouraged by the crowds on trains for further destinations.

Experiments with steam haulage in the early 1880s were unsuccessful and horsepower was reverted to in 1884 before electric traction was introduced in 1886. By 1927 the electric system was well and truly worn out and the Southern Railway, which had inherited the tramway in 1923, bought a pair of four-wheeled Drewry railcars to operate the service along with the existing trailers. One of these, the famous 'Grapes Car', was sent to Hull Transport Museum in 1937 when new trailers were built. Later the power cars were converted to diesel traction.

With the modernisation of the railway in the 1960s and the change to most trains using the former up platform at Esplanade, the relative convenience of the tramway greatly declined and with both stock and infrastructure becoming life-expired, BR decided to close the tramway. Considering how much of a contribution it had made to the town's transport until only recently, it expired with surprisingly little fuss in 1969. Its

derelict course can still be seen between the foot pier (now also used by cars) and the railway but few other traces remain. The remains of one of the Drewry cars was on site at Havenstreet at one time but has not been in evidence there for some years.

Saddler Vectrail

With the impending closure of the Ryde-Cowes line, the Saddler Railcar Co made a bid to take it over and operate it with light railcars, an early attempt at converting heavy to light rail.

The company, which established itself at Droxford on the closed Meon Valley line as a base and test centre, spent several years pursuing its scheme but sadly it was eventually to founder. The main problem, it later became clear, was not the unviability of the concept but the obstacles put in its way. The Island Council, while making encouraging noises, soon began to blow lukewarm at best, partly as the alternative of using the railway route through Newport for improved roads began to attract support. BR was officially neutral but behind the scenes some of its officers were quite malign. The problem faced by a number of preservation schemes at this time applied here too: 'If we could not run this railway, we're not going to let anybody else demonstrate that we were wrong!'

Eventually tiring of banging its head on this corporate brick wall, where every proposal was met with a plausible-seeming objection, Saddler Vectrail eventually gave up. It was this departure which allowed the Isle of Wight Steam Railway to negotiate a lease for Havenstreet-Wootton with the Island Council, by now owners of the freehold of the route, and obtain the track and other infrastructure from BR. All had to be done in a great hurry, as demolition started on the remaining sections within days of the preservationists removing their stock from Newport station. How attitudes were to change over 20 years!

A Comparison

Once or twice it has been suggested that there are interesting parallels and contrasts between the Isle of Wight and Isle of Man railway systems. Here are just a few thoughts.

Both served islands where the tourist trade was pre-eminent and were geared largely to the needs of tourism, on islands of similar-sized resident populations (although the Isle of Man has about twice the area). However, the Isle of Man Railway took this policy to a greater extreme, linking only the places where tourist numbers seemed likely to support its operations. Its use of a narrow gauge, its willingness to reduce its operations to almost a

token service out of season and its aggressive policy of buying out or buying into the competition, enabled it to remain profitable — just — into the 1960s.

Isle of Man visitors were equally captive and dependent on public transport; however, no service to the pierhead for them, not even a horse tram to Douglas station! They had a half-mile walk, their luggage hopefully following on behind. There they met another breed of Beyer Peacock locomotive, which hurried them to their destinations along single lines where no expense was allowed if it did not bring a positive result on the balance sheet.

But each railway served its island's needs well and enough of both systems remains for the enthusiast to be able to make his own first-hand comparisons and ponder which got it right or whether the contrasts were due to different circumstances.

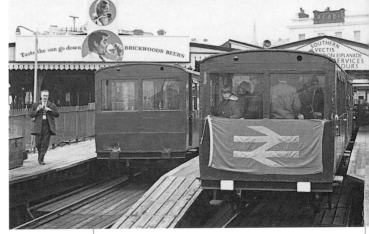

Above right:
26 January 1969 was the final day of tramway operation and the trams were decorated to mark the occasion. Both motor/trailer sets are seen at Esplanade station.
John H. Bird

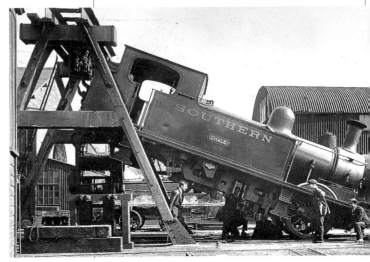

Right:
Despite its relatively small fleet, Ryde Works was — and had to be — self-sufficient almost to main works standard, which involved some ingenious solutions to heavy engineering problems. *Chale* is undergoing motion and axlebox repairs in 1929, suspended by a large hook from a wooden gantry. A common enough approach at small works at the time but a modern Health & Safety officer would probably have a fit!
O. J. Morris